Praise for *The Blame Game*:

"In a perfect workplace, credit would be given where credit is due . . . In reality . . . finger-pointing can become so rife it becomes almost impossible to determine what actually went wrong in the first place. That can erode trust and teamwork, and stifle creativity. Ben Dattner . . . believes that credit and blame lie at the psychological core of the workplace. He sees credit as a proxy for evolution, learning and adaptation and blame as a proxy for reactive, reflexive and backward-looking behavior."

—*The Wall Street Journal*

"Dattner delves into the psychological and cultural reasons we can't stop pointing fingers, providing tips so that next time you're in a high-stakes office situation, you'll recognize the credit/blame imbalances and think, 'recalculating'"

—*Psychology Today*

"Dattner explains the importance of de-emphasizing many employees' natural inclination to place blame on others and seek credit for themselves. By applying his suggestions, organizations can experience greater success."

—*Pittsburgh Business Times*

"By understanding our natural tendencies, how our organizations function, and leaders' effects on blame and credit, we can better understand and control our own reactions to the blame game. . . . If you're dealing with a culture that fosters blame at work—or if you're guilty of hoarding credit while hurling blame—Dattner has some strategies to improve."

—*Arizona Central*

"Dattner provides an eloquent account of the impact of credit and blame in our lives. . . . Whether you are a CEO of a Fortune 500 company, a consulting psychologist, or just beginning your first job out of college, *The Blame Game* will provide you with a sophisticated perspective on the dynamics of credit and blame."

—The SIOP Exchange

"Getting blamed for a screwup at work or having someone else take credit for something you've actually done can be frustrating, to say the least. But it can also spread deep inside a company, demoralizing staff and ultimately making work more about office politics than 'getting the job done'. . . . Dattner explains how these dysfunctional strategies can apply to young entrepreneurs and how thinking about credit and blame differently can lead to better results."

—Portfolio.com

"A failure to understand the dynamics of blame and credit at work can and will derail your career. Don't take my word for it. Read the overwhelming proof in *The Blame Game*. . . . a lean synthesis of how to manage the workplace toxin called blame."

—BNET

"Packed full of intriguing, all-too-familiar stories and based on a foundation of well-established theories and research, *The Blame Game* is an excellent resource for developing greater self-awareness about the dangerous allure of blame, and greater social awareness about the contagious effects. Ben Dattner provides us with sound practical advice about how to stop playing the blame game, and how to instead create and maintain relationships and organizations based on honesty, trust and respect."

—Annie McKee, coauthor of *Primal Leadership* and founder of Teleos Leadership Institute

"Blame and credit constitute a hidden economy that if not managed properly, can undermine even the most promising organizations and derail even the most promising careers. This book is an encyclopedia of blame in the workplace that anyone, at any level of their company and at any stage of their career, can benefit from reading."

—Keith McFarland, #1 bestselling author of
The Breakthrough Company and *Bounce*

"We've all suffered from the blame game, whether we are the one getting unfairly blamed or the one yielding to the temptation to unproductively blame others. Through the lens of organizational psychology, Ben Dattner explains why blame is so prevalent in the workplace and presents so many challenges in our careers. Then he shares practical advice for how to break free from the blame game by taking appropriate responsibility for our actions, learning from our mistakes, and giving others the credit they are due."

—Susan Nolen-Hoeksema, author of
Women Who Think Too Much and *The Power of Women*

"Through a wealth of stories and research, *The Blame Game* presents a compelling case that individuals, groups, and organizations can benefit greatly by focusing less on blame and more on problem solving and collaboration. Leaders at any level of any organization will find practical guidance for how they can make this shift and also lead others in a better direction."

—Pamela Meyer, author of *From Workplace to Playspace: Innovating, Learning, and Changing Through Dynamic Engagement*

"Ben Dattner has authored a brilliant and timely book. Unfortunately, the blame game is alive and all too well in business today. In *The Blame Game* the author offers us insights into how to change the game and create healthy and productive companies."

—Doug Lennick, coauthor of *Moral Intelligenc*

THE
BLAME
GAME

*How the Hidden Rules of Credit and
Blame Determine Our Success or Failure*

BEN DATTNER

WITH DARREN DAHL

FREE PRESS
New York London Toronto Sydney New Delhi

FREE PRESS
A Division of Simon & Schuster, Inc.
1230 Avenue of the Americas
New York, NY 10020

First Free Press trade paperback edition February 2012

FREE PRESS and colophon are trademarks of Simon & Schuster, Inc.

For information about special discounts for bulk purchases,
please contact Simon & Schuster Special Sales at 1-866-506-1949
or business@simonandschuster.com.

The Simon & Schuster Speakers Bureau can bring authors to your live event.
For more information or to book an event contact the Simon & Schuster Speakers Bureau
at 1-866-248-3049 or visit our website at www.simonspeakers.com.

DESIGNED BY ERICH HOBBING

Manufactured in the United States of America

1   3   5   7   9   10   8   6   4   2

The Library of Congress has cataloged the hardcover edition as follows:

Dattner, Ben.
The blame game : how the hidden rules of credit and blame determine
our success or failure / by Ben Dattner with Darren Dahl.
p. cm.
1. Organizational behavior. 2. Blame. 3. Interpersonal relations.
4. Management—Psychological aspects. I. Dahl, Darren. II. Title.
HD58.7.D356 2011
302.3'5—dc22   2010037570
ISBN 978-1-4391-6956-8
ISBN 978-1-4391-6957-5(pbk)
ISBN 978-1-4391-6958-2 (ebook)

NOTE TO READERS:
Names and identifying details of some of the people and organizations portrayed
in this book have been changed. In some instances, composites are used.

To my parents,
with love and credit.

Contents

Introduction

> All that most maddens and torments; all that stirs up the
> lees of things; all truth with malice in it; all that cracks the
> sinews and cakes the brain; all the subtle demonisms of life
> and thought; all evil, to crazy Ahab, were visibly person-
> ified, and made practically assailable in Moby-Dick. He
> piled upon the whale's white hump the sum of all the gen-
> eral rage and hate felt by his whole race from Adam down;
> and then, as if his chest had been a mortar, he burst his hot
> heart's shell upon it.
>
> —Herman Melville, *Moby-Dick*

After the collision with the geese, there was eerie silence: the
plane's two engines had failed. On January 15, 2009, U.S. Air
Flight 1549 had just taken off from LaGuardia Airport in New
York City.[1] Luckily for the passengers and crew, the pilot in
charge that day was not only highly qualified and well trained to
think under pressure, he also didn't let fear of being blamed get
in the way of the decision he was about to make. Captain Chesley Burnett Sullenberger III quickly realized that he must either
turn the aircraft around and try to land back at LaGuardia, possibly saving the plane, or try to land in the Hudson River, the
closest thing to an obstacle-free landing strip that was in sight.

The water landing provided the best odds of saving the lives of those on board, but it would surely ruin the aircraft: "Sully" decided to land in the Hudson, and all of the passengers and crew survived, with only minor injuries reported, making the news all around the world. As he said later, "I could have worried that my decision to ditch the plane would be questioned by superiors or investigators. But I chose not to."

This is the kind of autonomous and heroic decision we would all like to make in our work lives—but unfortunately, many of us find ourselves working in organizations or for bosses who blame people for the wrong things, for the wrong reasons, at the wrong time. Misplaced blame can not only lead to a great deal of frustration, anger, and ultimately disengagement from our jobs, but can also cause us to not speak up or take the right action when we should, for fear of retribution. The allocation of credit as well is often badly out of whack in many offices, with some people getting credit for our contributions or those of others that they don't in all fairness deserve. Someone makes a suggestion in a meeting which gets ignored, and then someone else makes the exact same suggestion a few minutes later and receives acclaim. Or everyone in an office cuts a certain corner in the way they do their work, but only one person gets blamed for doing so.

We see it everywhere: a CEO blaming his company's failure or troubles on his predecessor; an employee egregiously taking credit for a co-worker's idea or accomplishment; a government official referring to a huge unpaid tax bill as an "accountant's error" or an oil company official pointing the finger at every organization except his own in the wake of a disastrous spill. Just look out your office door or over your cubicle wall and you're likely to find a co-worker either trying to collect praise from you, your peers, or your boss for the invaluable contributions they've made or working hard to deflect blame—especially during tough times when everyone fears a single mistake could cost them their job. It wasn't the shipping clerk's fault that the customer didn't receive the order; blame the delivery company. You can't blame product development for the company's poor quarterly results—the fault lies clearly with the sales team. Listen in on any given conversation between two colleagues out on the street or at a restaurant in which someone is complaining about his or her job, and you'll find the discussion almost inevitably involves outrage about not getting fairly credited or resentment about getting unfairly blamed, and feeling unappreciated or persecuted. And while the tendencies to pull undue credit toward ourselves and push blame toward others are pervasive in our work lives, they are never more intense than at the worst possible time: when the stakes are high, times are tough, and trust, collaboration, and new approaches are necessary. How we handle credit and blame is also contagious; it can quickly have devastating and widespread effects throughout the workplace.

For example, I was once brought in by the CEO of a technology company to consult to a state-of-the-art scientific facility where world-renowned scientists and highly experienced administrators were locked in a cycle of blame. Their director had left to go work for a start-up, and the people he left behind were facing a budget shortfall as they tried to recruit a replacement. Far away from the CEO and corporate headquarters, those who worked at the facility felt neglected by management and were growing increasingly concerned that their division would be closed or sold. Rather than trying to work together and make shared sacrifices to protect their jobs, however, the scientists and administrators blamed each other for the director's departure and the worsening financial situation. The finger-pointing became evident even to the candidates who came in to interview for the position of director. Most left the building turned off by the toxic atmosphere and the way members of each of the feuding groups talked about the other. The dynamics of credit and blame playing out in this way worsened the budget crisis and lengthened the time it took to recruit a new director, creating a self-fulfilling downward spiral which put the survival of the laboratories in more doubt than ever.

As an organizational psychologist, I consult to organizations, large and small, for profit and not-for-profit, in the United States and abroad. Every time my phone rings, there is an individual, team, or organization on the line seeking assistance with issues relating to credit and blame. Whether it's a CEO wondering why his management team has become mired in finger-pointing and isn't getting along, or a financial analyst at a hedge fund worried she won't get a fair bonus, there has not been a single instance in which I have advised individuals, groups, or an organization where credit and blame was not a crucial issue, if not the single most important issue underlying their problems. I've learned through years of consulting with major corporations as well as by serving as National Public Radio's *Morning Edition* workplace consultant, that "the blame game"—the elaborate set of self-serving rules and subjective judgment calls which impact how we keep score of blame or credit for ourselves and others—is a key factor in whether workplace relationships are friendly and collaborative or harsh and unforgiving. The dynamics of credit and blame—and specifically whether we succumb to the blame game ourselves or learn to avoid its tempting allure—also have a great deal to do with how successful we will ultimately be. Within teams, credit and blame determine whether scapegoats will be identified and persecuted, or whether collective responsibility will be taken when things go wrong. Between teams, credit and blame dynamics can help explain why collaboration and trust are present, or why negative spirals of mutual recrimination are occurring. How credit and blame are assigned can even determine whether entire companies adopt a mindful view of their challenges and take necessary actions in order to move forward, or get stuck in dysfunctional finger-pointing and score-settling.

Many researchers have studied "management derailment," which occurs when managers' careers derail and they either fail in a job, or do not reach their full potential in an organization.[2] One key aspect that all such "derailed" executives have in common is that their halted progression was not their own choice—rather, something about how they acted led to their involuntary exit from, or demotion within, their organization. What the studies have found, for example, at the Center for Creative Leadership (CCL) is that a key factor in why managers fail is that they are poor at managing relationships: they fail to give proper credit to those they rely on, and yet find ways to blame others for their shortcomings.[3] As we'll explore further in chapter 6, how a leader attributes credit and blame can be a major determinant of whether that leader succeeds or fails.

Along similar lines, Howard Tennen and Glenn Affleck at the University of Connecticut School of Medicine's Department of Psychiatry analyzed the results from twenty-two studies conducted on the impact of blaming others.[4] Seventy-seven percent of those studies showed that when individuals blamed others, they were actually worse off for doing so—both emotionally and physically. In the remaining studies, there was no benefit for people when they blamed others, regardless of whether the person they blamed was a spouse, a physician, or a stranger. In other words, across all of the studies they looked at, blaming is ineffective at best, and more likely to be harmful. This study provides further evidence that despite the short-term temptations of blaming others, doing so doesn't help the blamer, and is even likely to be costly over the longer term.

A study conducted by Harvard Medical School psychiatrist George Vaillant showed that people who "projected," or blamed others for their misfortunes, were much less able to adjust to the changing events in their lives. As Vaillant writes, "No one is harder to reason with than the person who projects blame,"[5] and he labeled this tendency an *immature defense* because denial and extreme defensiveness should be more common to children and adolescents than to grownups. In another study, conducted by psychiatrist Leslie Phillips at Worcester State Hospital, it was found that the more people fell into the pattern of blaming others for their problems, the worse off they became in dealing with their life in general.[6] In other words, those who blame other people to an extreme extent pay a serious price for doing so.

I first learned about the importance of credit and blame when I worked at Republic National Bank of New York for three years in between college and graduate school, first as a management trainee and then as assistant to the CEO. As I rotated through different departments in the bank, I was fascinated by who got credited when things went well and who got blamed when things went wrong. One day, I noticed a piece of paper that a co-worker had tacked to his cubicle wall that outlined "The six phases of a project: 1. Enthusiasm 2. Disillusionment 3. Panic 4. Search for the guilty 5. Punishment of the innocent. 6. Rewards for the uninvolved." Despite having studied many formal academic theories of teams and team development since I first saw that list, I have yet to come across a more accurate description of how most dramas play out in our working lives. Unfortunately, in too many organizations, unfair and harmful credit and blame processes determine who gets rewarded or punished in a manner that is totally uncorrelated with actual talent or performance. As a result, creativity and productive risk taking can be crushed, and people may not feel confident making the tough decisions that need to be made. If a co-pilot fears being blamed by the pilot for insubordination, he may not speak up even as the fuel gauge reads empty or the altimeter indicates that a mountain is approaching. If an individual is too afraid of blame to experiment with new things in her career, it's unlikely she will ever blaze a new path or make a breakthrough contribution. If a team is more concerned with justifying performance than with improving it, team members will waste precious time and energy in searching for something or someone to blame instead of fixing problems or making progress.

I once consulted for a retailer that was opening new stores in the Southeast. Previously, the retailer had sold its goods in shopping malls, but now for the first time it was expanding by buying or building its own free-standing locations. When the expansion fell behind schedule, my job was to find out what had gone wrong with the team of managers assigned to choose and open the new locations. A deadline loomed, as an investors' meeting was approaching and the CEO wanted to be able to proudly announce the signing of leases in the new locations. As I interviewed the group members and they recounted the story, it became readily apparent what had transpired: the team had not delineated responsibilities or determined decision-making authority. It was unclear who would research new locations, or how the final decision as to which city, neighborhood, or location stores should be opened up in would be made. As a result, the team wasted weeks of time duplicating each other's research and arguing over which deals should be made, the whole time not knowing whether a simple majority, a unanimous vote, or even any kind of group agreement or consensus was necessary.

This inaction had finally spurred one team member, a young woman named Beth, to act unilaterally. She had the most experience in analyzing potential store locations, the deepest real estate knowledge, and had done the most research into specific cities and neighborhoods. She had grown frustrated with her colleagues because they would criticize her suggestions without offering any alternatives. Mindful of the deadline that the team was facing, and pessimistic about ever reaching a consensus, Beth began making offers on store locations and hiring architects to begin working drawings. At one meeting, as the team argued about where a store should go in one city's downtown area, Beth mentioned that she had already made an offer on a property in that city's suburbs.

After the shock of this announcement wore off, the other team members grew furious in response. They didn't perceive that Beth was just trying to do her job. Rather, fearing that she would make the rest of the team look bad, they interpreted her action as an attempt to get personal credit. In fact, Beth had no intention of claiming credit for the store openings; she was simply trying to move the ball forward. None of the other seven people had paused and asked the team to reflect on its goals, accountabilities, or processes. Instead, they joined together in making Beth a scapegoat, blaming her for the team's failure to meet their timeline. "Beth's mishandling of the location research has put us way behind schedule," they complained to upper management, adding, "We question whether she did enough analysis on the locations she selected."

When Beth learned about what her colleagues had done, she was completely taken aback. In her mind, she was the only one who had actually done anything to move the research and the dealmaking forward. She had thought it better to begin working on something rather than wait around, trying to "herd the cats," as she put it, and do nothing. Beth believed it was better to ask for forgiveness than to ask for permission. What she never anticipated was that by acting independently, instead of receiving credit for taking the initiative she became a convenient scapegoat for her colleagues to channel blame onto, for the team's failures.

In this particular organization, which was highly political, the other seven members of the team concluded that they had more to gain by blaming Beth for the delay than by working together to meet their deadline. Senior management called her in and demanded to know what was going on. While she could have told the whole story and argued her case, Beth had passed the point of no return. Within a few weeks, she quit her job and left the company. There was an initial sense of relief among her former teammates that she was gone, but the team soon had to confront its dysfunction because it remained unable to accomplish its task. A few months later, well after the critical deadline had been missed, I was called in by the CEO to assist the team with clarifying roles, responsibilities, and decision-making processes. Ironically, the company decided to open up stores in all of the locations Beth had selected.

Some organizations get it right, but in my experience it's a rare organization that hasn't had serious struggles with credit and blame. The challenge for most of us, unfortunately, is that we find ourselves slogging away in corporate cultures built on negative assumptions and vicious cycles of interaction, cultures based on fear and finger-pointing instead of trust and problem solving. Our office lives come to feel like a high-stakes game of "blame or be blamed."

Those who love their jobs will likely tell you that they feel appreciated for their talents and contributions, while those who dread coming to work will probably complain that they are unfairly blamed or do not receive their fair share of credit. Try testing this theory the next time a friend of yours says that she just loves her job. Ask her why she enjoys it so much. I've found that the answer will have more to do with how your friend relates to the culture where she works than with compensation—"My boss really appreciates my contributions," or, "I feel like I'm recognized and rewarded for what I do," or even, "I feel like my boss and my teammates 'have my back.'" Great bosses and colleagues are good at sharing due credit and do not assign undue blame, while awful ones use all kinds of mental gymnastics to distort, deny, or misremember facts and events in order to take credit and dispense blame.

The stark truth is that credit and blame matter. It's in our nature to care a great deal, often more than we should, about whether we are being fairly or unfairly credited or blamed. Each of us comes to work every day with a legacy of evolutionary hardwiring, early life experiences, acculturation, and socialization that significantly influence how we give and receive credit and blame. Our sense of pride, our ego, is easily offended when our bosses or peers fail to recognize our contributions. On the other hand, that same ego protects itself from feeling shame by building defenses against being criticized for a misstep. For both ego-enhancing and self-protective reasons, we can come to spend an inordinate amount of time and energy adopting self-serving and defensive positions. Because of human evolution and our own early life experiences, most of us care too much about how much credit we receive, and often fight to get credit even if it ends up costing us much more than it's worth. In other words, we tend to care more about building our self-esteem and enhancing our social standing instead of taking a longer-term view and acting in our pragmatic self-interest.

We can all benefit by learning to be more strategic about credit and blame. Consider, for example, how taking a step back and looking at the bigger picture might have helped Robert Kearns, an engineering professor and owner of the patent covering the invention of intermittent windshield wiper blades in cars. Kearns's story, first told in an article in *The New Yorker* and then in the movie *Flash of Genius*, starring Greg Kinnear, is a cautionary tale.[7] Kearns battled the giant car companies like Ford and Chrysler for years for violating his patent. What makes his story relevant is that he was so driven by the need to receive credit for his invention that he destroyed his marriage and his academic career, even suffering a mental breakdown.

It was on a rainy day in November 1962 that Kearns, a life-long inventor who had built prototypes of a hair gel–dispensing comb and a missile guidance system, among other things, had his moment of inspiration: why couldn't his car's wipers blink the way his eye could? Kearns then worked in his basement laboratory until finally coming up with a functional prototype, which he installed and tested on his Ford Galaxie. Kearns grew up and lived in Detroit, home of the Big Three auto giants—Ford, General Motors, and Chrysler—and he had seen other inventors get rich by supplying the automakers with their parts. Kearns intended to follow their lead. So he set off in his Galaxie on a journey to show off his invention. After receiving some interest from Ford and what he thought was a promise from Mercury, Kearns eagerly began testing and tweaking his new wiper-blade system, financing the whole project himself and asking his wife and four children to sacrifice along with him until their big pay-day arrived. But it wasn't really money that Kearns was after: he wanted the recognition that he, Bob Kearns, had invented something useful and he wanted to be publicly credited for that achievement.

The problem was that Kearns's payday didn't come for another thirty years—and even then not in the form he had longed for. After seeing his invention, the various automakers created their own intermittent wiping system, claiming they had come up with their design independently while basically telling Kearns to go away. Not surprisingly, Kearns was outraged, believing the automakers had stolen his idea. But, despite the hardship, he was not ready to give up. And so, for the next thirty years, using his children as his assistants, he mounted an incessant legal campaign against the automakers for infringing on his patented system. He even turned down huge settlement offers from the automakers. He wanted his day in court, so he could tell his story to a jury and the world.

The problem was that Kearns sacrificed just about everything he had on this quest—his marriage, his life savings, everything—to prove how wrong the car companies had been to steal credit for what he firmly believed was his idea. Kearns eventually won jury awards of more than $20 million from Ford and Chrysler—with lawsuits still pending against just about every other carmaker in the world—and yet he was still greatly disappointed. If he had been able to think more strategically, Kearns might have realized that his pursuit of credit as an inventor would paradoxically and tragically bring blame and suffering upon him in other realms of work and life.

We allow ourselves to be drawn into irrational credit seeking and the vicious cycle of the blame game in large part because we have a strong need to see ourselves in a positive light, even if that means ignoring or distorting important information that we should be aware of about our own talents and performance. Almost everyone holds him- or herself, or his or her group, to a different standard than others; it's human nature to do so. This is not a book about good and evil—though there are certainly cases where people blatantly lie and knowingly blame others for things that they themselves are responsible for or steal credit for things they know they had nothing to do with. Of more interest to us, because they are much more common, are situations in which people truly believe that they deserve more credit than they're due, that they are above blame, and that others should take the fall. These distorted beliefs cause them to get caught up in the blame game. How we claim or assign credit or blame to ourselves and others is a major determinant of whether we learn and grow in our careers or stagnate and derail. It also helps determine whether we are trusted and respected or resented and undermined by the people who work with or for us. The good news is that coming to a better understanding of the dynamics of credit and blame can bring a competitive advantage both to you in your career and to the team and organization you work in. I've found that when individuals, teams, and organizations learn to hand out credit strategically and blame accurately, they create a virtuous cycle where they not only perform better and learn more, but are also happier and get more satisfaction out of their work.

Understanding the dynamics of credit and blame for ourselves and others, however, isn't easy. It involves looking in the mirror and realizing that each of us sees the world through our own self-serving lenses and from our own familial and cultural vantage point. The feedback we may need to move forward in our careers isn't always positive, and the journey to the summit of credit often involves traveling through the valley of blame. I'll argue that there can be enormous benefits in reducing our daily credit intake and seeking out small, homeopathic doses of blame. In order to help you avoid the trap of falling into the blame game yourself, and to successfully engage with the credit-grabbers and finger-pointers in your work life, in the pages that follow we'll explore more deeply the evolutionary, psychological, and cultural reasons that the blame game is so alluring and pervasive. I'll describe how blame can quickly escalate, but will also share strategies for how to reduce and defuse it.

We'll first consider fascinating insights from the field known as evolutionary psychology. For example, we're not the only primates to be overly concerned with social life and organizational politics to the point where we ignore "reality." Vervet monkeys are so focused on who is dominating or appeasing whom in their groups that they often miss clues that there are predators in the vicinity.[8] Other mammals also pay close attention to reciprocal social interactions and relationships—for example, even bats credit and blame other bats in the way they share their food with one another.[9] We'll also explore how early life experiences come into play, considering how children learn to assign credit and blame, and see how, to some extent, whether we like it or not, or realize it or not, every day is "take your family of origin to work" day. We will also look at how gender and culture impact the way credit and blame are given and received by men and women, and by people from different cultures.

Then we'll take a close look at the egregious things bosses and colleagues do, and consider the underlying reasons why they do these things, revealing the ways in which individual personality, workplace relationships, team dynamics, and organizational cultures can predispose people to credit and blame fairly or unfairly. I will argue that successful individuals learn to navigate between the one extreme of pathologically blaming others for everything and the other extreme of blaming only themselves for anything. Developing empathy for why others are so prone to blame can help you blame them less, thereby stopping—or at least slowing down—the cycle of blame. As individuals, we all reach forks in the road where we can either veer toward accuracy or head down the tempting but slippery slope of self-serving rationalization. Examples of this include saying things to yourself like, "Maybe I should give Harry some credit here, but after all, I'm the one who really made this happen," or, "Yeah, I screwed up, but it was really my boss's fault; he didn't warn me about the things I needed to know." Whether we admit it or not, we all have powerful urges to rationalize this way. As Kevin Kline asked in *The Big Chill*: "Have you ever gone a day without a rationalization?" We can all help each other blame less and learn more.

Organizations also reach forks in the road where the thinking and behaviors that were rewarded in the past are no longer optimal in a changed environment. It's tempting to blame any individual or group that advocates change, especially since change requires taking a step back in order to take two steps forward. Prioritizing change and learning over the long term usually means that performance will suffer in the short term. Organizations with static patterns of credit and blame get stuck, rigidly defending the status quo because social dynamics and vested interests prevent progress. The more an organization is able to constantly readjust its internal dynamics of credit and blame to align with a changing external marketplace or environment, the more likely it is to survive and thrive. Closed organizations that suffer from dysfunctional politics, that credit people who defend the status quo, and blame anyone who challenges it, are going to be under increasing threat in our rapidly evolving "open," "open source," and "networked" world. If an organization doesn't fairly credit talented people for their ideas, skills, and contributions, another organization or network will. Thanks to the Internet and other technologies, organizations are transforming from centralized hierarchies to decentralized networks. Open organizations constituted by networks in which people trust and credit one another fairly for contributions, and blame each other proportionately when warranted, will ultimately triumph over closed, overly political organizations. In today's world, networks determine which Hollywood movies will be successful, who will host *Saturday Night Live*, and whose travel video will become a YouTube sensation and cross over to the Discovery Channel. Organizations that are trapped in the blame game will have a hard time adapting to this new world.

In order to stop playing the blame game, individuals, teams, and organizations have to learn how to overcome their tendencies to think and behave in habitual ways and learn to take a new, adaptive, and counterintuitive approach. Some hospitals, for example, have learned that rather than hiding behind lawyers and denying their mistakes, they are better off standing up and admitting their responsibility for errors—spending their resources to correct problems instead of trying to conceal, deny, or obscure them. Not only can this help doctors and nurses learn and prevent similar errors from happening again, which saves lives, but the hospitals have also found, perhaps surprisingly, that the families of patients harmed or killed by an error are less likely to sue when the hospital steps up and takes the blame. We'll explore when and how taking blame and owning up to your mistakes can create more opportunity for improvement than denial ever could, despite the risks of doing so. We'll also consider how CEOs and other leaders can create either positive or negative cultures in which the dynamics of credit and blame dramatically enhance organizational learning or in which they tragically constrain it.

In my experience, people who enjoy their jobs or who lead high-performing teams and organizations have learned to pay close attention to the social psychology of credit and blame, and to build a firm foundation for collaboration and problem solving. As one example, a real estate developer hired me to conduct "partnering" sessions for the architects, engineers, and managers who were about to begin construction on an innovative "green" building. The developer, who had many years of experience in all kinds of building projects, told me that he found that bringing people together at the beginning of a project was a great way to avoid the blame game, since it is all but inevitable that the temptation to point fingers would emerge over time. An insightful and enlightened leader of his family-run organization, he knew that it was important to address the social psychology between groups in advance, just like any other kind of project planning. He wanted to create an environment of trust in which people would fix rather than blame. By establishing the foundation for collaboration, he could greatly increase the odds of achieving a successful outcome. Then, as problems came up, the groups acknowledged their own oversights, and constructively helped each other solve problems. Well-managed credit and blame helped the teams create a building that broke records for its low environmental impact. Just as he helped build a "sustainable" building, the developer helped build sustainable trust and collaboration between all of the teams involved in the design, construction, operations, and maintenance of the building.

It's very rare that anyone ever became a "great boss" without demonstrating some mastery of the ways in which credit and blame can so powerfully influence motivation, workplace relationships, and teamwork. When credit and praise are assigned fairly, it triggers an impulse in every member of the organization to elevate their performance. And if, while working for a great boss or at a great organization, someone makes a mistake, he or she is likely to stand up, disclose, and take responsibility for their error because they know that if they acted in good faith they will be forgiven and encouraged to try again. Because they are less afraid of being punished for errors of "commission" or speaking up, people working in great organizations are much less likely to make errors of "omission" by remaining passive or silent. When credit and blame are managed properly, people are willing and able to experiment, learn, and grow. When credit and blame are mismanaged and unfair, people shut down, become demotivated, and focus more on covering their rears than on moving forward.

The challenge is to rethink our evolutionary hardwiring, early life experiences, acculturation, and socialization, so that we can do a better job ourselves of avoiding the blame game and can contribute to building the kind of office environment where everyone thrives. In my role as an executive coach and organizational development consultant, I have never been able to help an executive, team, or corporate client if I haven't effectively challenged their beliefs about credit and blame, illustrated how dysfunctional patterns have created or reinforced the status quo, and helped them change their narratives of, and assumptions about, credit and blame. My job is to help my clients identify the underlying causes of and stop vicious cycles—and then to help them make the changes necessary to start and reinforce virtuous cycles. Although my specific mandate may be to help the organization select higher-potential employees, to coach an individual, to mediate a conflict, to work with a single team or multiple teams, or to help the organization change its culture, I'm not able to do any of these things without encouraging people to think about how they are making sense of credit and blame, and to explore alternative narratives and strategies.

It's my hope that after reading this book, the next time you find yourself navigating a high-stakes workplace situation, instead of taking the nearest exit you will hear your own internal voice say, "recalculating." This book is all about how recalculating and reevaluating credit and blame can serve as a positive force for individual learning, workplace relationships, and team and organizational dynamics.

In chapter 1, we'll look at how nature, through evolution, has shaped how people assign credit or blame to themselves, considering how we all tend to give ourselves undue credit when things go well and to shirk responsibility when things go badly, from individuals overestimating their contributions to group projects to CEOs making rationalizations in annual reports. In chapter 2, we'll focus on nurture—how our family experiences, gender, and cultural influences shape our ways of thinking about, and behaving in regard to, credit and blame. In chapter 3, we'll examine how personality and personality types impact how individuals assign credit or blame to themselves and others, considering how tempting it is for certain kinds of people in particular to hold others to a different standard and to cast blame away from themselves. Then, in chapter 4, we'll explore how situations have a powerful but often underestimated influence on how we perceive and react to credit and blame. Chapter 5 is all about corporate cultures and how credit and blame is a key component of these cultures, for better or worse. In chapter 6, we turn to leadership, and show how the way in which leaders assign credit and blame, and the atmosphere that they create, influences their success or failure as well as the success or failure of the organizations they lead. And chapter 7 builds on the preceding chapters to suggest practical ways in which individuals and organizational leaders can increase the chances that credit and blame will be a positive force for change and growth rather than a negative force for stagnation and failure.

Let's get started.

CHAPTER 1

The Nature of
Credit and Blame

The Beatles were angry and upset when they thought that someone else was getting the credit they deserved for their psychedelic eighth album, *Sgt. Pepper's Lonely Hearts Club Band*.[1] They felt they had been underappreciated because *Time* magazine had described the record as "George Martin's new album," crediting their producer.[2] Martin had famously played a key role in defining the band's sound, and for this new album he had experimented with new techniques in sound mixing which contributed to its groundbreaking nature. Although the album went down in history as one of the greatest ever recorded, this story illustrates just how fraught credit and blame issues can be. Even the Beatles, despite all of their success and fame, had difficulty sharing credit.

Across all human cultures, and throughout all of human history, keeping close track of credit and blame has been considered vital. Many religions have concepts of a system of divine accounting, or a "book of life," wherein God or the gods keep track of one's good and bad deeds in order to determine reward or punishment, either in this world or the next. Even for people who do not believe in any such divine, cosmic, or karmic judgment, the principle that we should receive due credit for our good intentions or good deeds and not be unfairly blamed holds powerful sway.

THE HIGH COST OF CREDIT

So powerful, in fact, is our desire to receive due credit that we sometimes demand it at what might be considerable expense. A friend of mine, whom I'll call Pria, took me out to lunch one day to ask for some career advice. Pria was preparing for an upcoming meeting with her boss, Larry, in order to talk about her future at the nonprofit think tank where she works. Pria had worked very hard over the last year and knew she was being underpaid in her role. She also resented that she had the same title as the two people who reported to her. As we discussed her game plan over lunch, Pria told me that she planned to begin the meeting by expressing her dissatisfaction with her title, and then to make a strong argument for getting a promotion. She would then talk about her compensation, which she knew from research about comparable organizations was about $20,000 lower than that of her counterparts.

During our discussion, it became clear to me that Pria cared more about the title than about the salary. When I asked her if this was the case, she readily agreed, saying, "I lose credibility with outsiders because I have the same title as the people who report to me." But I was skeptical. In the more than twenty years I've known her, Pria's charisma and intellect have impressed anyone she's met, both personally and professionally. Her title wouldn't have been more than a footnote to any conversation. I decided to press the issue, asking her if she could think of a single example of a situation in which she'd lost credibility. After thinking it through for a moment, she admitted she couldn't. I then asked her whether she felt Larry valued her. This time she answered without delay, saying, "No, he doesn't." While Larry heavily relied on Pria to ghost-write articles and speeches for him, he never publicly acknowledged that she was providing most of the "thinking" that powered the think tank he had founded.

The real reason why Pria wanted the promotion had little or nothing to do with what she had called "optics" to outsiders. Instead, the promotion had everything to do with her feeling undervalued in her role by Larry, who had originally recruited her from a prestigious private-sector consulting firm. I asked Pria to make a hypothetical choice: Would she prefer a new, more prestigious title or a bump in pay that would bring her in line with her industry peers? In other words, would she "buy" a promotion if that possibility were offered to her? Thinking about it, she realized that the money would actually be much more beneficial for her than the new title. Pria had been "suboptimizing," caring more about the perceived meaning of something— which, in this case, was the "credit" that a promotion would have symbolized to her—than about her substantive economic interest. Pria's case is a good example of about how this bias toward receiving credit can play out in our work lives in our relationships with our bosses. Working for a boss who gives us what we consider to be fair credit is something that people are willing to "pay for" in a variety of ways. In my experience, having a good relationship with one's boss—defined in large part by the fairness with which one's boss allocates credit and blame—is actually as important as a 25 percent difference in salary. Many people are willing to forgo higher compensation in order to have a boss who makes them feel respected and valued. I often challenge my clients, as I did with my friend Pria, to consider the potential trade-offs between symbols and substance. However, for many of us, it's hard to determine what is symbolic and what is substantive, and we can blame our innate confusion on evolution.

BRED FOR CRED(IT)

We are all vulnerable to falling into traps regarding the allocation and distribution of credit and blame because, as crucial as fair judgment is to us, disagreements about who deserves credit or blame are the norm and agreement the exception. Why is this the case? A good number of our default actions and reactions can be explained by human evolution.

In recent years, researchers in evolutionary psychology have made notable progress in explaining ways in which the survival pressures that ruled our earliest ancestors' lives have shaped our thinking and our behavior: for example, why we gorge ourselves on fatty foods and sweets; why we often misperceive risks, as in the recent subprime mortgage fiasco; and why racism lingers even when we imagine ourselves to be equal-opportunity and enlightened. Many of our ways of thinking and behaving have roots back in the African savannah, and our tendency to over-zealously keep track of credit and blame also began there.

This tab-keeping seems, in fact, to be a deeply hardwired feature of the animal kingdom. Consider the research conducted on chimpanzees and capuchin monkeys by two biologists, Sarah Brosnan and Frans de Waal, at the Yerkes National Primate Research Center in Atlanta, who investigated how animals react to inequities.[3] The scientists conducted a series of experiments in which the monkeys and chimpanzees could trade tokens—small rocks or pieces of pipe—for food. While some of the animals received bits of cucumber or celery in return for their tokens, others received tasty grapes—which might be the equivalent of a co-worker getting a promotion or a raise while you got, well, a piece of cucumber. When the animals, which had previously been quite content receiving celery, saw that others were receiving grapes, they literally turned their backs to an offer of a treat like cucumber. Some monkeys went so far as to toss the cucumber back at the researchers in fits of rage.

In addition to the analogy of relating to our compensation and our bosses that these primate cousins provide, we can learn lessons about how we relate to our co-workers from an unexpected branch of our extended mammalian family tree—bats. Researchers have studied bat behavior and discovered that bats, like humans, track reciprocal social relationships. One study focused on the aptly named vampire bats, which inhabit regions of Central America and feed at night on the blood of large animals.[4] If a vampire bat misses a meal, it can turn to its "co-workers" for help. Once bats return to their dens each night, those lucky enough to find food that evening will regurgitate blood into the mouths of their less successful colleagues. What's really interesting is that vampire bats have an innate sense of fairness and reciprocity and keep track of who has been generous and who has been greedy. If a bat has been denied a favor by a fellow bat, it will refuse to share with that same stingy bat in the future. As we'll discuss further in chapter 4, people also pay close attention to reciprocal social relationships, and keep careful track of how they are credited and blamed by co-workers.

John Stacey Adams, a workplace and behavioral psychologist, developed *equity theory* in the 1960s to explain why and when workers feel they have been treated unfairly, and to predict how they will react when they perceive inequity.[5] Adams found that employees seek to maintain equity between the inputs that they bring to a job (such as time, effort, and personal sacrifice) and the outcomes they receive from their employer (like salary and recognition). According to Adams's equity theory, our innate sense of what is fair also relies heavily on a comparison of our inputs and outcomes with the input and outcomes of those around us. If we're working our tails off and fail to get the promotion we feel we deserve, and at the same time we see that a lazy co-worker lands a plum position, there's a good chance we'll do something equivalent to turning our backs on, or even throwing the cucumber in the face of, our boss. When we perceive inequity, stinginess, or a lack of reciprocity on the part of colleagues or the organizations we work for, we are much less likely to collaborate and much more likely to try to find ways to somehow right the wrongs that we feel have been done to us.

BLAME YOUR BRAIN

Due to the much greater and more numerous threats to survival that our ancestors were subject to, our brains have evolved to make quick, unconscious decisions. They have also evolved to simplify matters in order to facilitate a speedy response in the face of too much information. Over time our species was wired to use mental shortcuts, such as relying on past experience to judge future outcomes, and the result has been that our perceptions are influenced by what psychologists call *cognitive illusions*. These are subconscious mental maps that often get in the way of accurate or rational assessments. As the psychologist Daniel Gilbert writes in his book *Stumbling on Happiness*: "We feel as though we are sitting comfortably inside our heads, looking out through the clear glass windshield of our eyes, watching the world as it truly is. We tend to forget that our brains are talented forgers, weaving a tapestry of memory and perception whose detail is so compelling its inauthenticity is rarely detected."[6]

We are also a good deal less in command of our thoughts, and our actions, than we tend to believe we are. One illuminating study even showed that when we perceive we are making a conscious decision, our unconscious brain is way ahead of us. The researchers found that they could predict if a subject was going to press a button or not a full seven seconds before the subject reported having made the decision.[7] While this kind of experiment has yet to test when we unconsciously make decisions about credit and blame before we are aware we have done so, the implications are clear—our subconscious is in the driver's seat.

We still have our ancient brains, and they may be driven to perceive and act without reflection. This is why in the middle of a particularly complicated or emotional situation, such as an imminent layoff at the office, we and our co-workers may act like we stepped right out of the Stone Age.

One way in which our evolutionary programming leads us astray is that trustworthiness and fairness have become so important to us that we have come to prioritize fairness even when it conflicts with our "rational" self-interest. This is demonstrated powerfully by something called "the ultimatum game," an experiment designed by German economists in 1982.[8] Two players are given a sum of money and told to split it up between them. One player is given the power to split the money and to decide how much he and the other player will get. The other player then has the chance to either accept or reject the offer. If the second player decides to reject the offer, neither player receives anything. Rationally, the second player should accept any offer he is given; at least he'll receive *something*. But what researchers who have conducted this experiment countless times in cultures all around the world have found is that when the offers slide out of balance, moving from a fifty-fifty split to, say, an eighty-twenty one, the second player will reject the offer. Just like the capuchin monkeys who threw their cucumbers after grapes caused wrath, people would rather receive nothing than be subject to a raw deal. Our emotional primate hardwiring trumps our rational economic self-interest.

Another way in which our brains distort our perceptions and behavior is by leading us to give ourselves more credit for successes than we're due and to downplay our responsibility for failures. This behavioral trait was termed "beneffectance" by psychologist Anthony Greenwald,[9] derived from the combination of "beneficence," doing good, and "effectance," or competence. He defined it as "the tendency to take credit for success while denying responsibility for failure." A number of studies have shown that people, particularly Westerners, overcredit themselves for everything from how much they have contributed to group efforts to their skill at public speaking to how much they will be missed at a social event they can't attend. Studies have also shown that if you ask each member of a work group to estimate what percentage of the group's work output he or she contributed, the total adds up, like the fictional shares sold in the Broadway musical *The Producers*, to much more than 100 percent.

Most of us also have wildly optimistic views of our futures, where we believe that due to our interpersonal skills and intellectual gifts, we are more likely than our peers to have a happy marriage or a successful career. Psychologists term this trait *illusory superiority*, a cognitive bias where people overestimate their positive qualities and underestimate their negative ones. It may be better known as the *Lake Wobegon Effect*, inspired by the fictional town where, according to Garrison Keillor, "all the children are above average." Keillor's point, of course, is that everyone tends to see him- or herself as above average. As the psychologist Steven Pinker writes in *The Blank Slate*:

> People consistently overrate their own skill, honesty, generosity, and autonomy. They overestimate their contribution to a joint effort, chalk up their successes to skill and their failures to luck,

and always feel that the other side has gotten the better deal in a compromise. People keep up these self-serving illusions even when they are wired to what they think is an accurate lie detector. This shows that they are not lying to the experimenter but lying to themselves. For decades every psychology student has learned about "cognitive dissonance reduction," in which people change whatever opinion it takes to maintain a positive self-image.[10]

As Bertrand Russell noted: "Every man, wherever he goes, is encompassed in a cloud of comforting convictions, which move with him like flies on a summer day."[11]

Ironically, it is often the least talented among us who are the most likely to overcredit their contributions and abilities. Consider for example a study of college students conducted in 1999 by Justin Kruger and David Dunning of Cornell University.[12] The researchers tested the students for their aptitude in logic, grammar, and humor, and then asked the students to self-rank—to guess at how they would stack up against their peers. What they found was that students with the lowest scores most overrated themselves, believing they were more skilled than they really were, and assessing themselves far above their actual ranking.

Our natural tendency to delude ourselves and to be legends in our own minds doesn't stop here. We also prefer to think that our positive traits strike much closer to the core of who we are than any negative aspects of our personality. So, when a friend or co-worker describes us as "a hard worker" or "a good listener," we say to ourselves, "Yes, that's me." But when we read in our annual performance review that we "tend to lose focus" or that we may be "too social with our co-workers," we tend to get angry and defensive—even accusatory. This can occur even when the evaluations we receive are entirely credible.

SERVING OUR SELVES

The distortions of "beneffectance" fall within a larger category of *self-serving biases*, subconscious processes by which we assess our capabilities and achievements in a distorted, overly positive manner. We basically trip over ourselves in pursuit of praise and credit but conveniently find a way to blame external causes—anyone and anything—for our failures. This tendency even applies to organizational leaders. There have been numerous studies around the world dating back to the early 1980s that have investigated how senior executives make self-serving attributions all the time to protect their self-image and their reputation—either by claiming credit for positive results or by deflecting blame toward external and environmental factors for negative outcomes.

In one of the most influential of these studies, researchers Gerald Salancik and James Meindl found that management teams frequently used self-serving attributions in letters to their shareholders.[13] Management teams generally attributed the firm's good fortune to their contributions and were three times more likely to fault the environment for setbacks than they were to take responsibility for them. In the same vein, if a manufacturing company has a bad year, the temptation is to blame anything from a depressed economy to an influx of cheap foreign imports rather than the management of the firm. On the flip side, when external factors beyond a management team's control, such as a fluctuating currency or a rebound in consumer demand, have had a strong role in improving a company's bottom line, the company and its CEO will likely find a way to show how the improved performance was instead a direct result of their smart decisions and flawless execution.

In another study, researchers found that entrepreneurs tend to take credit for the success of their business—citing internal factors such as their work ethic or management skills—while blaming external factors like taxes and the scarcity of available financing when their business struggles or fails.[14] Outside observers believed that those same outcomes were actually the result of internal factors such as an entrepreneur's lack of planning or strategic vision as opposed to a poor economy or onerous government regulations. The study involved asking two samples of entrepreneurs to name the factors they believed had contributed to or impeded the success of their businesses. One sample was composed of 189 pharmacy owners and the other of 231 owners of small businesses, which ranged from antique stores to travel agencies. The researchers also recruited a panel of sixteen business "experts"—a group composed of professors of entrepreneurship, graduates of an MBA program who majored in entrepreneurship, and business counselors in a college-based entrepreneurship center—and asked them the same two questions about the success or failure of small businesses. The results showed that both the entrepreneurs and the experts largely attributed success to internal factors.

When it came to identifying what causes businesses to stumble or fail, however, there was quite a divergence in explanations. Entrepreneurs believed that 84.1 percent of the reasons for their struggles were factors external to their business, with government regulation and the labor market ranking as the two most common answers. The experts, on the other hand, attributed 72.6 percent of a business's struggles to the internal personality characteristics of the entrepreneur, which included work ethic, knowledge, and dedication.

Self-serving attributions can be a mixed blessing in terms of both self-esteem and social esteem, the regard one is held in by others. On one hand, taking undue credit for good outcomes and denying blame for bad outcomes is a tempting short-term strategy for protecting one's self-esteem. The potential downside of this approach, though, is that unrealistic credit-takers do not develop a true assessment of their contributions and capabilities over the longer term. Similarly, there can be a short-term temptation in taking undue credit or even denying due blame as a means of building social esteem. In the short run, someone who conveys a high degree of certainty about his creditworthiness and a conviction that he is not to blame for anything of importance, may convince others that there is truth to those self-serving attributions. However, over the longer run, if someone develops a reputation as a credit hog or an unfair blamer, the social esteem in which others hold him may take a precipitous dive.

A relevant area of psychology known as *attribution theory* casts interesting light on how our brains are able to convince us of the veracity of our self-serving self-assessments. Simply put, attribution theory describes the patterns by which we explain the causes of our own versus others' behavior. There are actually two broad kinds of attribution: *personal attribution*, which is when we explain the actions of ourselves and others based on ability, personality, mood, or effort; and *situational attribution*, which tries to explain behavior by invoking contextual or environmental factors. For example, if your boss stomps into your office and snaps at you for something particularly minor and petty, you might call him a jerk once he's left the office. "How dare he talk to me like that," you might think to yourself. "He's really bad at keeping his emotions under control, I can't believe such a hostile person ever got promoted." That's personal attribution in action because you've explained your boss's behavior based on some particular personality trait you have ascribed to him. You could also, though, have taken into account factors other than your boss's character that might explain his behavior. Perhaps you knew he was having trouble at home or that his own boss had just chewed him out earlier in the day. Then, you might have thought, "I can tell he's upset about something else, but I wish he wasn't taking it out on me," taking his outburst less personally.

When it comes to ourselves, we also have a choice of what factors we attribute our behavior, or our success or failure, to. It's easy to succumb to the temptation to use inconsistent explanations for good and bad outcomes. For example, we seek to collect credit for our successes based on a personal attribution—"Of course, I deserved that promotion; in fact, it was overdue"—but use situational attribution to distance ourselves from failure—"I didn't get that promotion because the boss has always had it in for me." In one study that demonstrates this dynamic in action, psychologists Kathryn Saulnier and Daniel Perlman from the University of Manitoba asked both prison inmates and their counselors to explain why the prisoners had committed their crimes.[15] What they found was that the prisoners blamed situational factors for their incarceration; the counselors, on the other hand, thought that the prisoners themselves were to blame.

Consider a situation where your company loses an important customer that you were responsible for working with. In this case, you are likely to blame the loss of the account on something situational, like budget cuts at the customer's company, but your boss might attribute the loss to you personally, arguing that you did not follow up often enough. On the other hand, where we might see a co-worker as rigid, we see ourselves as resolute. And, when a colleague makes a mistake in, say, placing a purchase order, we are quick to blame and criticize her for it even though we personally have made the same exact mistake many times. When we did it, we might have said to ourselves, "It's not my fault; the process is broken."

REFLEXIVE BLAME

Because of self-serving biases and double standards, we tend to not only favor ourselves but also to be biased against others. Our own decisions and behaviors make perfect sense to us, while those of others are often irksome, and we are quick to blame them. As David Foster Wallace, the late novelist and author of *Infinite Jest*, explained in a commencement speech to the Kenyon College class of 2005, "A huge percentage of the stuff that I tend to be automatically certain of is, it turns out, totally wrong and deluded."[16] As Wallace suggested, we tend to see the world too narrowly through our own eyes, not taking into account other people's perspectives and situations, and we jump to conclusions about why they are behaving as they do. In his speech, Wallace speculated that perhaps the driver of that SUV that just cut you off didn't do it to try to kill you. Maybe he's the father of a sick child rushing to the hospital, and you were blocking his vehicle, not the other way around. It comes naturally to simplify other people's situations and motivations, and then to blame them for the motivations we ascribe to them. We seem to have programming that leads us to be quick to accuse others, for a variety of reasons. As deeply bred into us as self-preservation is, so too are impulses to scapegoat and blame others.

Consider the story of Koko (her real name, unlike most of the other individuals mentioned in this book), the gorilla living in captivity in California who reportedly has learned one thousand words of sign language as a way to communicate with researchers. One night, Koko broke a toy cat she was playing with.[17] When asked by her scientist keeper the next morning what had happened, Koko quickly signaled that it was her nighttime attendant who was to blame. Koko, like early humans, automatically blamed someone else for her misstep because she feared retribution and possibly rejection from her "tribe"—in this case, the group made up of her keepers. Our ancestors would have known that rejection by their tribe would have meant certain death. Even our primate predecessors learned the not-so-subtle art of pointing the finger of responsibility elsewhere.

Scapegoating is an ancient practice, one found throughout history and across cultures. The term itself has its origins in the biblical Jewish ceremony of Yom Kippur, where the sins of the people are symbolically transferred to a goat that is then sent away into the wilderness.[18] Over our history, humans have constantly embraced rituals that involve transferring blame for something gone wrong to everything from clay pots to snakes and a menagerie of other animals and, quite often, to other humans. Sir James Frazer, the Scottish anthropologist and author of the twelve-volume classic *The Golden Bough*, published in 1890, labels such rituals "the transference of evil." As he writes (with the mind-set of the colonial period):

> The notion that we can transfer our guilt and sufferings to some other being who will bear them for us is familiar to the savage mind. . . . Because it is possible to shift a load of wood, stones, or what not, from our own back to the back of another, the savage fancies that it is equally possible to shift the burden of his pains and sorrows to another, who will suffer them in his stead. Upon this idea he acts, and the result is an endless number of very unamiable devices for palming off upon someone else the trouble which a man shrinks from bearing himself.[19]

Frazer recounts dozens of odd and often bloody scapegoating rituals performed by ancient man. When Arabian tribes were suffering from a plague, they would lead a camel through the village so that the animal would somehow absorb the pestilence. They would then take the camel to a sacred place and strangle it.

When cholera struck the ancient villages of Central India, every resident would retire to his or her house at sunset. The village priests would then parade the streets, plucking a straw from the roof of each house, which they would burn along with an offering of rice, ghee, and turmeric. The priests then daubed chickens with vermilion and drove them in the direction of the smoke, hopefully carrying the disease along with them. If the chickens failed, the priests tried again, using goats and then pigs.

When the Aymara Indians of Bolivia and Peru were suffering from a plague in 1857, they loaded a black llama with the clothes of the plague-stricken people, sprinkled the load with brandy, and turned the animal loose into the mountains, hoping that it would carry the sickness away with it. In the Middle Ages, animals were even put on trial for their misdeeds—from beetles who dared to chomp the wood inside a church to a locust that devoured a farmer's field to a pig who decided to bite a drunkard who had fallen into a ditch. As Julian Barnes describes in *Nothing to Be Frightened Of*:

> Sometimes the animal would be brought before the court, sometimes (as with insects) necessarily tried in absentia. There would be a full judicial hearing, with prosecution, defence, and a robed judge, who could hand down a range of punishments— probation, banishment, even excommunication. Sometimes there was even judicial execution: a pig might be hanged by the neck until it was dead by a gloved and hooded officer of the court.[20]

HUNTING WITCHES

We have also, of course, often scapegoated people, both individuals and whole groups. Think of the strange events in the upstart religious colony of Salem Village, Massachusetts, in 1692. Tragically, over the period of just a few months, more than a hundred men and women were accused of practicing witchcraft and cavorting with the devil—all of it started by accusations leveled by two young girls. In the end, nineteen people were hanged on Gallows Hill (five more, including an infant, died while being held in prison). The sequence of events raged out of control like a wildfire, almost consuming the Puritan movement with it, all within a year.[21]

Salem has continued to draw the attention of historians over the past three hundred years. By painstakingly putting together key pieces of evidence, such as letters and diary entries penned at the time, they have shed much light on the factors that led to the frenzy. Their conclusions reveal a sobering tale about how individuals, groups, and even whole cultures can turn on others, including their own members. Those living in Salem were in a society where war was a constant threat; each new day could bring a surprise attack from the Native Americans, who greatly outnumbered them. The threat of deadly diseases was also rampant, and neighbors eyed each other warily for signs of infection. Meanwhile, the local economy had collapsed and anger had built up toward the wealthier members of the community. A rigid and inflexible moral code woven into everyday life was haphazardly enforced. When combined, all of these elements added up to a powder keg of fear, distrust, and resentment that only needed a simple spark to ignite it. Fear—particularly of forces that we can't see or completely understand—is a great motivator of scapegoating, and evolutionary psychologists and other commentators tell us that witch-hunts, metaphorically speaking, are hardly a thing of the past.

When the news broke in March 2009 that several dozen executives at American International Group (AIG), the finance and insurance giant, had collected some $165 million in bonuses on the heels of the company's fantastic collapse,[22] you could almost hear the gasp around the country—quickly followed by a torrent of outrage: "How dare they!" After all, AIG received the money as part of the federal government's "bailout" of many of the big Wall Street Firms. There is clearly an argument to be made about whether those executives did or did not deserve the money (call them retention bonuses if you will, but most editorials and public opinion as a whole sided with *did not*). But more relevant for our purposes is to consider that while AIG was certainly one of the key players in the economic house of cards that imploded, the causes of the crisis were much more complex than any one factor or organization, and many parties contributed to it. But regardless of how complex and multifaceted the reasons for the collapse, the country suddenly had this one company in particular to point the finger at. As Kathleen Hall Jamieson, an expert in political communication, told a *New York Times* reporter: "Under these circumstances, you have victims and you need to find a villain."[23]

One of the great dangers of the tendency to scapegoat is that it diverts attention away from broader, deeper problems in societies or organizations, such as the structural, cultural, economic, demographic, or technological shortcomings of a system or an enterprise. Researcher Jo-Ellen Pozner has studied how businesses often deflect blame for corporate misconduct by making their employees into sacrificial scapegoats. She says that companies are driven to blame low-level employees for high-level dysfunction or for larger structural problems that might exist throughout the company. "It's very convenient to have a couple of people who are easily identifiable, it's easy to use them as a scapegoat to protect the reputation of [the companies]," she told a reporter for the *San Francisco Business Times*.[24]

Just as members of various groups have been historically persecuted or purged, corporations these days often demonstrate the same kind of primitive response to threats, whether in the form of poor earnings, internal dissent, or increasing competition. Entire departments may be outsourced or replaced in a manner that makes no economic sense. In fact, management experts have argued that layoffs often don't help the bottom line and advocate alternative ways to cut head-count expenses, while arguing that many organizations end up having to hire back employees under different arrangements at greater cost.[25] Nonetheless, when times are tough, companies continue to yield to the primitive instinct to purge departments, or assign disproportionate blame to particular individuals or groups. Too many leaders miss opportunities to identify and fix the real, but usually subtle and complex, causes of losses or failures. Scapegoating is a convenient way to increase cohesion in the short term, but the first victims of scapegoating are rarely the last. Scapegoating anyone in an organization ultimately yields harmful social dynamics and cultural risks that threaten everyone.

STEREOTYPING

As a species, we are all too ready to go along with the tide of blame, and there are a number of powerful subconscious processes through which our brains determine who we will attach blame to. Unfortunately, it's rare that organizations ever blame the right people for the right things, for the right reasons, at the right time, in the right way.

One of the disturbing ways in which individual people and whole groups are singled out for blame is through *stereotyping*, whether based on ethnicity, gender, or personality type. This is a mechanism that, once again, was bred into us over the course of evolution. In ancient times, stereotyping helped us speed up our decision making in life-or-death situations. Is that creature staring at you from across the river going to want you for its lunch? If the creature was a fellow human, failing to quickly identify him as a member of an enemy tribe would have been what we call in contemporary workplace-speak "career limiting." In our distant past, friends were friends, foes were foes, and there weren't fine gradations or distinctions in between. No matter how enlightened and equal-opportunity we imagine ourselves to be, unconscious stereotypes still influence how we evaluate people and situations.

Consider what the Harvard psychologists Anthony Greenwald, Debbie McGhee, and Jordan Schwartz learned when they created what is now known as the Implicit Associations Test, or IAT, in the late 1990s.[26] When you take the test online (which you can do at https://implicit.harvard.edu/implicit/), you are asked to match up or "associate" words with pictures that are flashed on your computer screen. The test measures how quickly you make those connections. Although several varieties of the excercise are available—such as ones based on gender, sexuality, or age—the test that measures racial stereotypes is the best known. In this version, you are shown faces of white and black people and then asked to label them with either positive words like *trust* or negative ones like *crime*. You basically take the test twice: first, you are asked to associate "good" words with the pictures of white people or with ones of black people, and then it all repeats with "bad" words. What the results reveal is the common time delay in linking black people with positive words—which means that many people have an unconscious bias that links black images with negative terms. The same is true of connecting white people with positive words. Therefore, for the majority of people, it's easier to make faster associations between white and good and creditworthy, and bad and black and blameworthy. How you score on the test, however, will depend a lot on your own racial and social background, and whether you yourself are a member of a minority.

Thankfully, there are legal, ethical, and cultural reasons why demographic group memberships are "protected classes" in the American workplace. And despite lingering sexism and racism, most organizations have incentives to provide equal treatment to, even if not equal opportunity for, all of their workers. However, as we'll explore later, the people in accounting and the folks in HR can still interact as if they were Croats and Serbs, or Hutus and Tutsis. And there's no law protecting the equal rights of HR or accounting. We all have to be wary of this kind of group warfare within companies, and take care not to make unjustified associations between people and attributes simply because they are members of a certain group, or because they happen to have, or play, a certain role.

MISTAKEN IDENTITY

In December 2009, CBS announced that it would be canceling *As the World Turns*, the long-running daytime soap opera. Eileen Fulton had played the character "Lisa," one of TV's first villainesses, a woman who was married nine times, divorced frequently, and even widowed on several occasions, since the show got its start in 1960. Originally cast as the sweet little girl-next-door, Fulton says that over time she steered Lisa to the dark side and embraced her role as a character everyone loved to hate. But what's on point for us is that the fans of the show apparently had a hard time distinguishing between Fulton the actor and Lisa the character—an association that actually became so dangerous that Fulton had to hire bodyguards. As she told an interviewer on National Public Radio's *Morning Edition*:

[The fans] love to hate me. But you know how it really began was I was standing on the street corner in front of Lord and Taylor's and this elegant woman came up to me and she said, "Aren't you Lisa?" And I thought, "Oh, my first autograph." I said, "Yes, that's the character I play." And she said, "Well, I hate you," and she hit me. And that was the beginning. I thought, well, this is kind of scary. But at least it was a compliment to the acting.[27]

Fulton's "fans" in this case were falling prey to an attribution error which caused them to judge Fulton as being bad or evil based on the behavior of her fictional character. The same principle might hold true for someone like Alex Trebek, the host of the game show *Jeopardy!* According to the official *Jeopardy!* website, Trebek holds two philosophy degrees from the University of Ottawa. While Trebek is likely an intelligent person, some fans might forget that when he corrects a contestant for an incorrect response, he already has the answers.[28] And Trebek didn't even write the questions himself: he has an entire staff that does that. (Incidentally, *Jeopardy!* writer and research positions are coveted and turnover is among the lowest of any job, anywhere: one writer, Steve Dorfman, was credited for having written more than fifty thousand clues for the show.)[29]

Psychologists Lee Ross, Teresa Amabile, and Julia Steinmet of Stanford University used a game show simulation in 1977 to study what Ross termed the *fundamental attribution error.*[30] Subjects were randomly designated as either contestants or hosts. When asked to evaluate the other participants in the study, contestants thought that the hosts were more intelligent even though they were aware they had been assigned randomly and had been instructed to make up their own questions.

The point is that it can be easy to fall into crediting or blaming people simply because of the role they are playing, whether that role is game show host or chief financial officer. Many CFOs I have coached over the years complain that they are viewed as cold and calculating simply because they are tasked with keeping close tabs on corporate spending. Most attorneys in the role of general counsel feel like they are seen as rigid, inflexible, and demanding because they are responsible for ensuring that the letter and the spirit of applicable laws and regulations are followed. Sometimes, managers and executives who are brought in as change agents end up encountering too much resistance from the organization, and they become concerned that they will be blamed for a status quo that they are unable to change. In some organizations, women feel like they are set up for failure by being given too many challenging goals to achieve and too few resources to achieve them, and then are scapegoated when they can't do the impossible. Some refer to this dynamic as the "glass cliff" that women risk falling off if given the "opportunity" to break the glass ceiling.

TRUTH TELLERS BEWARE

Although the advice to "separate the person from the problem" is wise and helpful in theory, it is hard to do in practice. Because of our evolutionary hardwiring, we tend to associate individuals and groups with problems quickly and conclusively. Those who speak unpopular truths, who publicly challenge prevailing wisdom or their boss's rationale, or who sound alarm bells about unacknowledged internal or external threats to an organization, may find themselves scapegoated and blamed for problems they did not cause, but simply tried to warn others about. Consider this illustrative example of one man who spoke too quickly and almost got himself fired by a CEO who didn't appreciate his honesty. Bart had been the director of compensation and benefits at a global manufacturing organization for six years. He was appreciated by his colleagues for his no-nonsense style and his willingness to work hard to bring in the best talent with competitive pay packages. One day, in a presentation to the CEO and the compensation committee of the board of directors, an external director asked Bart how the compensation of the company's senior management compared to that of comparable organizations. "We're definitely at the high end of the range, probably substantially higher than the average, and our increases have outpaced those of any other company," Bart answered. This was factually true, but Bart immediately realized that he had said too much and had made a political mistake. He had forgotten that the people whose compensation he was talking about, the senior management of the company, were in the room.

What happened next is an all-too-familiar story in the workplace. The CEO, an eminent elder-statesman type, had risen through the ranks over the course of twenty years. He had never particularly liked Bart, but now began to actively dislike him and to develop negative associations about him. During meetings over the following weeks, the CEO avoided eye contact and asked Bart all kinds of picayune questions and then impatiently cut him off as he tried to provide answers. It is likely that the CEO did not even consciously realize either that he had been angered by Bart's statement in the meeting or that he was treating Bart any differently than he had in the past. During this time, Bart's boss, Steve, had his annual performance review. The CEO gave him a "meets expectations" rating rather than the "exceeds expectations" he had received each of the four preceding years. When Steve asked about the basis for his rating, the CEO told him, "You haven't effectively managed Bart and now you need to get rid of him."

Bart was at high risk of being a scapegoat for several reasons, having to do both with his role and with his personality. People who are in charge of compensation and benefits in most organizations tend to be lightning rods for all kinds of negative associations and projections from others in the organization. Many people feel undercompensated and blame their boss or human resources for being cheap and unappreciative. Bart also willingly embraced the role of "messenger," and although he didn't enjoy taking anyone down a peg by letting them know that they over-estimated their "market value," he made no apologies for his estimates of what people were worth. Bart believed in "speaking truth to power."

Unfortunately for Bart, the CEO himself was insecure about his compensation relative to his performance and worried about his future at the organization. He had unconsciously perceived Bart's answer to the board member to be critical and disloyal of him. Bart was lucky to have Steve as a boss, because Steve had strong principles, prized fairness, and was good at managing the situation with the CEO. Steve argued that Bart's performance had been good, while acknowledging that he could improve in some areas, which he pledged to help Bart work on. Knowing that the turning point had been the compensation committee meeting, Steve also knew that it would serve no purpose to try to enlighten the CEO and to tell him that he had observed a change in his perceptions and behavior toward Bart. And Steve knew better than to challenge the CEO's reality by arguing that Bart was being unfairly scapegoated. Steve instead told the CEO that he would coach Bart on his "delivery skills" in order to make sure that his style was appropriate to the situation at hand, and he asked for six months to help Bart be more successful. The CEO reluctantly agreed.

Unfortunately, many of us are not lucky enough to have a fair and protective boss like Steve to shield us from unfair scapegoat-ing. One of the ways in which we can protect ourselves from becoming scapegoats is to learn to be more attuned to how what we say, and when and where we say it, might make us a target. It's helpful always to carefully consider the political risks of chal-lenging the status quo, or an organization's established "articles of faith." We should also be on alert for scapegoating others in these ways ourselves. This behavior is all too easy to fall into and it can lead to serious but avoidable problems, both for others and ourselves.

BECOMING MORE AWARE

Our best hope for counteracting the many automatic biases and impulses that have been bred into us, both by the long process of evolution and by our specific upbringing, is to become more cognizant of the powerful pull they have on us. Recognizing that our mental maps are preprogrammed increases the chances that we can learn to navigate the workplace in a new way. We need to constantly question our assumptions, and monitor our behavior, to make sure we're not reacting or acting out in a way that is more appropriate to the savannah than to the office. We should also regularly check in with trusted colleagues and mentors or coaches to get their perspective on how we are doing, and what we might do differently or better.

It is critical to strive for balance in terms of how we react to credit and blame. On the one hand, successful people gain a healthy degree of self-esteem and sense of identity from their contributions and social standing in the workplace. Caring about getting personal credit, and helping others do so, while avoiding blame for oneself and one's colleagues can be very motivational. At the same time, it is possible to care too much about getting credit and avoiding blame. Having too much of one's identity wrapped up in work can paradoxically lead to worse results if it makes people too anxious or hard driving. In *The Hero with a Thousand Faces*, Joseph Campbell described the archetype of the reluctant hero, who heeds the call to adventure, but with some trepidation in doing so.[31] As in many areas of work and life, the "middle path," in this case between caring too much and not caring enough, is the best one to take.

The rest of this book will describe the reflexive ways in which people assign credit and blame, and respond to credit and blame, and how these default actions and reactions can create problems in the workplace for individuals, teams, and entire organizations. I'll then argue that becoming mindful of the habitual ways in which we all give and get credit and blame is the first step toward replacing potentially dysfunctional reactions with more constructive and adaptive responses. I will also suggest ways to hear, but not succumb, to the siren song of unduly crediting ourselves and unfairly blaming others, which, while seductive, can derail careers and destroy companies.

CHAPTER 2

The Nurture
of Credit and Blame

Just as our primate and human evolutionary heritage exerts an invisible force on our perceptions and actions in the realm of credit and blame, so too does our own personal evolution—our family experience, as well as our gender and the culture we grow up in. All of these influences shape our behavior in the workplace and the kinds of roles we take on there, and they help determine how we dole out credit and blame to ourselves, as well as to our bosses, subordinates, co-workers, and rivals.

For a child, credit may be the most important kind of social reward, and blame the most important kind of social punishment, that he or she receives. How we receive credit and blame early in life significantly sets the stage for how we react later in life. We begin to learn about, and care a great deal about, credit and blame as young children, and our perspective tends to be one of extremes; we come to believe that we deserve all kinds of praise from our parents and teachers, and we also think that we're blamed unfairly all the time. "It's not fair" is one of the most primordial human complaints. As we get older, our understanding generally becomes more nuanced. When we mature, we begin to perceive that attributions can't always be made in a clear-cut manner, and realize that at times we may even be beneficiaries, not just victims, of the imperfect world of credit and blame. The problem is that, under stress, we can find ourselves inadvertently regressing to childish patterns. I sometimes tell my clients, only half-jokingly, that part of my job is to help organizations move from second-grade dynamics to something closer to tenth-grade dynamics, or to help prevent tenth-grade dynamics from devolving back to the second grade.

To understand how this kind of regression can occur, we need to look back at what we came to learn about praise and blame as children. As the late sociologist Charles Tilly, author of *Credit and Blame*, put it:

> We learn about credit and blame as children, though without being told that this is what is happening. From early on, parents blame their children for misdeeds, praise them for accomplishments, and take credit for their good qualities. Kids pick up the message by expecting credit when they accomplish something, but also by blaming others when they can. We grow up demanding credit, avoiding blame if possible, ourselves in turn blaming and giving credit in myriad ways.[1]

Our experience as children tends not only to mold our personalities in general but creates unconscious templates or scripts that influence how we react to and dispense credit and blame as adults. If you came from a home where you received lavish praise for your accomplishments, you may have developed stronger self-esteem and feel more comfortable bestowing credit on others. But you might also be too strongly in need of praise, which is so often lacking in the office. Many studies have shown that praise is in short supply in today's workplace, and that most managers miss opportunities to motivate their teams with credit and recognition. In *The Carrot Principle*, Adrian Gostick and Chester Elton presented a ten-year study involving more than two hundred thousand people that showed how much more effective the "carrot" of praise is than the all-too-common "stick" of blame.[2] In today's workplace, there is a challenging collision between the decreasing supply of praise and the increasing demand for it. Many recent graduates now entering the workforce have a much higher need for praise than did members of previous generations, and this can cause problems. University of Massachusetts education researcher Marilyn Lopes describes the potential pitfalls of having too strong a need for praise:

> A child who is praised too much may fall into the great-expectations trap. These kids feel the only way they can be accepted and loved is to keep performing at higher levels. Too much praise can also set up a fear-of-failure scenario. Kids are so dependent on the approval of others, they may be afraid to take risks. Scared that they won't be able to do a task perfectly, they don't do it at all.[3]

This problem may be especially pronounced for members of Generation Y, which the *Wall Street Journal* called "The Most-Praised Generation."[4] Many of my baby boomer and Gen X clients have marveled to me that their younger employees seem to think that they deserve a gold star simply for showing up to work each day. My colleagues at NYU still recount the story of one new student, who asked during an orientation to the master's program in Industrial and Organizational Psychology where I teach, "What kind of job will I *receive* when I graduate?" Several clients have told me that they linked this generational attitude in the workplace to the broader culture. For example, the change of language during the Academy Awards from "And the winner is . . ." to "The Oscar goes to . . . ," so that no one needs to feel deprived of credit or like they "lost" the Oscar. When Gen Y'ers enter the workforce and expect to receive frequent kudos and praise from their Gen X and baby boomer bosses, they are often quite disappointed at how rarely this happens. It is sometimes a revelation to recent college graduates that their bosses may, in fact, be pleased with their performance at work but don't shower them with praise. For a member of Gen Y, the absence of praise may feel like a boss is dissatisfied or disappointed.

It's not just the amount of praise one received as a child that matters, it's also the kind of praise. In a series of experiments, Stanford professor Carol Dweck and her colleagues found that children react differently when praised for their intelligence versus their efforts.[5] Those praised for intelligence may develop a "fixed" mind-set, where they believe that they possess innate abilities, while those praised for effort tend to develop a "growth" mind-set, believing that it is within their power to do better. In the face of setbacks, children and adults with fixed mind-sets are more likely to get demotivated and discouraged than those with growth mind-sets. After all, if intelligence or the ability to successfully complete a task is fixed, then if you fail at a task it must mean that you lack ability and can't do anything about that. In contrast, kids with a growth mind-set credit or blame their own efforts for success or failure. John Ryan, the president of the Center for Creative Leadership, where I'm an affiliate, told me and a group of fellow CCL executive coaches during our orientation that after he learned of Dweck's work, he has made sure to praise his grandchildren for how hard they worked on the paintings they made for him, rather than on how well the paintings turned out. Ryan believes that focusing on developable skills rather than on innate talents is equally helpful to the CEOs and other senior executives who attend programs at CCL.

The key point about the influence of our family experience is that as children we develop our sense of self, as well as our sense of where we fit into our families and the larger world, largely as a function of the credit or blame we receive. What others tell us we do well—or not—helps determine who we come to believe we are. A colleague of mine, counseling psychologist Brian Schwartz, has counseled thousands of people over the last thirty years, helping them to identify and pursue their career passions. He told me that in his experience, the people who are most fulfilled in their careers are people who are performing tasks that would have gratified them as a child, whether building, healing, helping, drawing, painting, or other such pursuits. Schwartz encourages his clients to think of their careers as huge portfolios of "ings" (activities). Among the most important for many of us in our jobs are "connect-ing to," "trust-ing," "collaborat-ing with," and "support-ing" one another. People who are happiest with their workplace relationships are those who feel credited by their colleagues for their knowledge or skill. Being picked to present to the board of directors may not be the same as being picked to play on a kickball team, but to most of us, it *feels* the same.

Our relationships with co-workers in particular can sometimes contain the same fulfillments and frustrations we experienced in our families of origin, including situations where we feel that bosses, like parents, favor us over our co-workers, or vice versa. For better or worse, when a workplace circumstance pushes our buttons, it's likely because it echoes an early experience in some way. Psychologists call this *transference*, meaning that we transfer feelings or emotions we had as children to someone we encounter in our adult lives. So, a boss becomes a pseudo-parent and a teammate a pseudo-sibling. When we unconsciously attribute family members' characteristics to co-workers, or when a situation at work reminds us of an early life experience, this can greatly diminish our ability to think clearly or act rationally in general, or when it comes to assigning and reacting to credit and blame in particular. If a boss begins to feel like a critical parent, or a performance appraisal like a report card, things can get interesting very quickly.

I counseled one client, a financial services executive, who was initially unaware that he was harshly blaming one of his employees because she had triggered angry feelings from his early family life. "So you're my parole officer?" he asked me when I arrived for our first meeting. The reason why I was there, according to the human resources department which had called me in, was that this brilliant executive lacked "emotional intelligence" and was a "brutal boss" to his staff. The HR department asked me to coach him on his management style, and to help him better manage and lead.

I asked him why he thought of me as his parole officer. "HR thinks I lack emotional intelligence," he replied. "My emotional intelligence is fine, dammit. I never wanted to manage anyone, but they assigned staff to me over my objections. Now that I'm not Mr. Nice Boss, they come down on me as being a jerk with no interpersonal skills. I have a ton of emotional intelligence and no need for a coach. The whole idea that I need coaching is a political setup."

So I asked another question. "Why don't we set aside emotional intelligence for the time being and instead discuss the politics here?" After I said this, he relaxed and began to talk about the politics at the organization. Indeed, there was an element of politics at play in the fact that he was being coached; there almost always is. One could even argue that in many cases, when an executive coach's phone rings and the person on the other end of the line is not the potential client, the coach is being asked to address a "presenting problem," which is actually a symptom of deeper and more complex organizational issues.

I asked the executive what had happened to prompt HR to call me, and he explained that as a result of a recent merger, he had been made a manager and now had to supervise a staff. Most of them went about their business and left him alone, but there was one of his direct reports, a woman based in Europe, who was endlessly annoying to him. She was anxious about her job, and constantly contacted him to check in, well beyond what he thought was necessary. He tried to be patient and politely reassure her that everything was fine, that he was satisfied with her work, and that he would prefer she send him final work products rather than asking him to sign off on each draft she produced. One day, when he was in the middle of a complicated financial model, she called him and asked him a question that, in his view, she either should have been able to answer or could have easily looked up herself. He got so annoyed he told her to stop bothering him and then hung up on her. This prompted her complaint to human resources about his brusque and unfriendly management style.

At our second meeting, I asked him the basic questions I ask all my coaching clients as I begin work with them—to describe any formative experiences that may be relevant to their perceptions and behavior in the workplace. As he began to describe his early life, it quickly became apparent to both of us why he had been so angry at his staffer. He described how upon arriving in this country, his parents had settled in an immigrant community in New England. He and his four younger siblings lived in a small house in which they shared bedrooms and had very little peace or privacy. He was the only sibling with any academic interest or talent, and he described how the one place in the house where he could spread out his papers while doing his homework was the dining-room table. There he would work all afternoon, trying to tune out the constant ruckus made by the brothers and sisters around him. From time to time, they would bother him even more by demanding help with their homework. So there it was. In this pristine corporate campus, with its well-ordered rows of offices and cubicles, he felt like he was being interrupted in his "homework" by his staffer, who became just like an annoying younger sister to him. Because of this unconscious association, he disproportionately blamed her and "acted out" in a way that was hurtful to her and harmful to himself.

I have found that such transferences from our family experiences are very common. Sometimes the transference can be positive; workplace relationships can be warm and supportive; and the office can feel like a cohesive family. However, too often it is negative dynamics rather than positive dynamics that get played out. An article by Michelle Conlin in *BusinessWeek* in 2004 titled "I'm a Bad Boss? Blame My Dad" was one of the first to cover the topic of transference at work, and how it can lead to serious dysfunction.[6] She describes a high-technology executive who lost his temper when a colleague's questions and challenges in a meeting made him feel like he was under siege exactly as his parents had made him feel during his youth. His perception that he was being blamed caused him to act out in a way that his superiors found much more blameworthy. Like many other executives and managers who derail, his psychological reaction to blame was a bigger cause of his difficulties than was the original criticism, real or imagined, he was initially defending against. This kind of overreaction can sometimes be the psychological equivalent of the canary in the coal mine, indicating that greater difficulties will soon follow.

A 2008 article in the *New York Times* by Sarah Kershaw also covered how family dynamics get reenacted in the workplace. Three clients of mine—Terry, Amy, and Gina—who own and run an advertising agency called TAG Creative, described how they each reenact their respective family's dynamics at work. Terry and Amy are both firstborns, with self-described "dominant" personalities, while Gina is a more diplomatic middleborn. Amy at times feels competitive with her partners, and came to recognize that she is reenacting sibling rivalry originally experienced with her sister many years ago. As Amy told the *Times*:

I feel there are moments where you are sitting there and you can feel it in your body, you're having a reaction, something gets triggered . . . it took on so much more import than it needed to . . . and this is not really about Gina or Terry or what they are doing in this moment, this is reminding me of something that happened a long time ago that gets acted out there.[7]

I worked with all three women to help them see how they were bringing "baggage" to work, so they could be more mindful about their interactions, and bring the best elements of their past experience into their partnership while leaving the less productive parts behind. Each of them came to "own" more of their respective "stuff," which made them blame each other less and work together more effectively.

THE BLAME-DEPRESSION CONNECTION

A particularly troubling way in which our upbringing can negatively impact how we contend with issues of credit and blame is by instilling in us an unhealthy understanding of the causes of positive and negative events in our lives. These attributions, in turn, can both cause and be a result of depression. And, in a vicious cycle, being depressed can further reinforce negative ways of thinking about the problems we're experiencing, making it even harder to cope.

People who are depressed are more likely to blame themselves for things that are going wrong. They demonstrate what psychologists call a *depressive attributional style*,[8] which is the tendency to overattribute blame for bad events to their own internal shortcomings rather than to external circumstances or events. People who are depressed are also likely to feel that bad situations and negative emotions are permanent rather than transitory, and that this negativity pervades their entire lives, rather than just certain aspects. A depressed person, for example, might say to herself, "It's my fault I'm not succeeding. I've always been unsuccessful and I will always be unsuccessful, and I'm unsuccessful at all aspects of my job and in all other areas of my life." Whether one's attributions for good or bad outcomes are "internal" versus "external" or "stable" versus "unstable" is often a result of how one has been credited or blamed by others in the past, particularly in one's early life.[9]

Depressed people have suffered a partial or full breakdown of the self-serving biases and illusions described in the last chapter. Sometimes depressed people can be more accurate than non-depressed people in the attributions they make, a phenomenon known as "depressive realism." It's hard to untangle which comes first and causes the other, attributional realism or depression. More likely, they go hand in hand, and are both influenced by early life experiences. And parents may play a key role in this.

Some recent research has uncovered a link between parental blame style and the incidence of depression among children and teenagers. This connection seems to cement itself between the ages of twelve and nineteen, which is the age group that researchers from the Institute of Psychiatry at King's College London studied when they collected data from 1,300 sets of twins to examine the link between parenting style and depression.[10] The researchers found that the more harshly punitive parents were toward their children, the more likely their children were to become depressed, to develop depressive attributional styles, and to internalize blame. And the effects can be long-lasting, as research by Jill Hooley, a Harvard psychologist, has demonstrated.[11]

Using magnetic resonance imaging machines, Hooley studied how the brains of women who had suffered from depression handled criticism from their mothers. When confronted with criticism similar to what they had been hearing for years—whether about tattoos, a lack of religious observance, or for simply being inconsiderate and untidy—the brains of women who had suffered depression showed activity in deep emotional areas rather than in the areas responsible for rational, analytical thinking. Women who had not been depressed showed activation in the more rational and analytic parts of their brains when criticized. When the experiment was run with the women receiving praise rather than blame, those women who had suffered depression didn't react as strongly as the ones in the control group, indicating that, as Hooley told *Harvard Magazine*, "It's as if they aren't getting the full benefit of the praise."[12] In other words, for women who had been depressed, praise was received as superficial and transitory while blame was experienced as deep and enduring. Conversely, women who had not been depressed were able to receive criticism without overreacting to it, and to experience more positive emotions when they were praised.

Other important research has shown that being subjected to continual blaming can lead to a state of mind called *learned helplessness*, identified by the University of Pennsylvania psychology professor Martin Seligman and his colleagues.[13] They have conducted many studies over the years which examine the relationship between how we account for good and bad events, and which have indicated a strong link between internal attributions of negative events and learned helplessness. In this state of mind, we come to believe that we've lost the ability to positively influence events or outcomes. If we have been blamed too much, for too long, we may begin to internalize blame and even start blaming ourselves unnecessarily. What Seligman found was that in the presence of prolonged exposure to blame—such as being criticized by a boss for bad outcomes at work or being found guilty by association without being given the opportunity to respond or fix things—humans can shut down. People may also begin to blame themselves, faulting the core of who they are, as in, "I am a bad person," or, "I messed everything up again."

The problem is that the more you begin to blame yourself rather than those external factors, the more hopeless you can become, because you don't believe you can, for example, stop one of your co-workers from always finding a way to blame you for their mistakes. The result is that people lapse into apathy, inactivity, a loss of motivation, and pessimism, and they can never escape the labyrinth of blame and self-blame. Unfortunately, this state of mind is also self-reinforcing. If we believe that we will be unfairly blamed for bad work outcomes, and will not be duly credited for good outcomes, we may well stop trying to do a good job. As our performance suffers, we find further evidence that we can't do our jobs well, and get stuck in a downward spiral. Getting blamed when we first start a job can cause self-perpetuating problems long afterward, just as being blamed early in life can challenge us even into adulthood.

Does this perhaps mean that we should turn to blaming others as a way out of this psychological quicksand? If self-blame can lead to depression, and depression can lead to self-blame, is the answer simply to begin blaming other people and external factors around us? The short answer is no—though if you do engage in such behavior, you might actually feel better at first as you externalize blame rather than blaming yourself. Blaming others can be energizing when one harnesses anger or righteous rage and may prevent depression caused by self-blame, but this strategy tends to backfire and prevent learning and growth over the long run. Ultimately, successful individuals focus less on the relative apportionment of blame and instead focus on fixing things in order to reduce the overall level of blame in their lives and careers. And, as in other areas in life and work, it can be harder for women than men to find the right balance.

CREDIT, BLAME, MAN, WOMAN

Gender can greatly impact how one is credited or blamed by others; how one reacts to the credit or blame that one does or does not receive; how one credits or blames oneself, and even how one estimates how much credit or blame one is receiving from others.

Despite the fact that we live and work in a supposedly enlightened era, stereotypes of women remain prevalent in the workplace and beyond. Female managers are still discriminated against when it comes to hiring decisions, evaluations of managerial and leadership performance, task assignment, and compensation. In fact, in addition to getting less pay for the same jobs, and less credit for the same accomplishments, women may also internalize their undervaluation, suffer more from self-blame, and have a harder time crediting themselves than men do.

The different pattern of attribution for women, in which they receive less credit and are more susceptible to self-criticism, may also be a partial explanation for why women are twice as likely to suffer from depression as are men. A ballpark estimate cited in the *New York Times* is that one in eight men will be depressed at some point during their lifetimes, versus one in four women.[14] There are a number of physiological, psychological, and social factors that contribute to this discrepancy, but it's possible that differential patterns of credit and blame also play a role. When a woman is passed over for a raise or promotion, she may suffer from *behavioral self-blame*, where she blames herself for not working hard enough, rather than blaming her boss or her organization for not recognizing her contributions. However, the real reasons she was not promoted may be that the organization, or maybe even prevailing societal gender biases, are at fault. There are many fewer women in high-profile corporate leadership positions than men, and in 2008 the U.S. Census Bureau reported that women are underpaid compared to their male counterparts by about 23 percent—a discrepancy that, among other factors, is likely partly due to unequal opportunity and partly because of unequal valuation of women's efforts.[15] The results of this survey indicate that women may get less credit than men in the workplace, and need to work harder than men to publicize their accomplishments in order to get the credit they are due. Unfortunately, because of their socialization, they may have a hard time doing so.

As communications expert Peggy Klaus relates in her book, *Brag! The Art of Tooting Your Own Horn Without Blowing It*:

> Although I've coached an equal number of males and females, and find that bragging is difficult for both genders, the majority of women with whom I work struggle with this issue far more than men do. It's a well-researched fact that women are terrible promoters. Told by parents and society at large, "Don't be a show-off," "Don't upstage your brother," "Don't talk about your accomplishment—it will make your boyfriend/husband look bad," women are less likely to draw attention to themselves and take ownership of their successes. They tend to attribute their accomplishments to other people, their families, or a work team. That's all very nice, but it's those who visibly take credit for accomplishments who are rewarded with promotions and gem assignments.[16]

Part of the explanation for this finding may be that women not only undersell themselves, they also underestimate how others evaluate them. One study found that female managers are three times as likely as men to underestimate how their boss perceives their job performance. The researchers surveyed 251 male and female managers from different industries across the United

States. Participants were asked to rate their own performance in nine areas—communication ability, initiative, self-awareness, self-control, empathy, bond-building, teamwork, conflict management, and trustworthiness. They were also asked to estimate how their supervisors would rank them. The results showed that the men slightly overestimated how their boss would rank them, while the women underestimated how their performance would be evaluated by 11 percent. The results were even more pronounced for women older than age fifty who began their careers in a more gender-biased era.[17]

CULTURAL HERITAGE

Our nationality or ethnic heritage may also play an important role in the ways we think about and react to credit and blame. Cultures provide guidance about what is important versus irrelevant and praiseworthy versus blameworthy, and teach us how to think about, and respond to, issues of credit and blame. In some cultures, slurping one's noodles is viewed as a positive credit to the cooking skills of one's host, while in others the slurper may be blamed for being rude and uncouth.

Some path-breaking research on cultural differences was done by the Dutch psychologist Geert Hofstede.[18] He tried to quantify some of the variations between cultures and how they influenced dynamics in the workplace by studying employee values scores from seventy countries collected by IBM between 1967 and 1973. Hofstede's goal was to help understand the kinds of cultural influences an employee might bring into the workplace; he formulated five key dimensions that varied between cultures, which he called Power Distance; Individualism; Masculinity; Uncertainty Avoidance; and Long-Term versus Short-Term Orientation. Each of these dimensions can provide a perspective on how cultures influence patterns of credit and blame.

For example, Power Distance describes how hierarchical a culture is. In a low Power Distance culture like Austria, Ireland, or the United States, a subordinate is more likely to feel comfortable speaking up or challenging a superior than someone from a high Power Distance culture like Malaysia might be. In his book *Outliers*, Malcolm Gladwell claims that plane crashes might be more likely in high Power Distance cultures like Korea or Colombia because co-pilots' fear of being blamed for challenging a pilot causes them to not speak up forcefully enough when the plane is in danger.[19] Gladwell then discusses how Korean Air learned from crashes and provided training to crews that taught them to more openly challenge one another despite their cultural tendency to be deferential. As we'll see in later chapters about organizational culture and leadership, great organizations and leaders encourage and foster cultures where people do not fear speaking up, pushing back, or experimenting with new approaches, even when doing so threatens the status quo.

The cultural dimension of Individualism versus Collectivism also has an important influence on credit and blame. In an individualistic culture like the United States, credit and blame are assigned to and by individuals, while in collectivistic cultures like China and Japan, credit and blame are assigned to and by groups.[20] Interestingly, in collectivistic cultures there are still "self-serving" biases, except that these biases favor one's group rather than oneself. We will explore in chapter 4 how even in individualistic cultures, members of groups can favor their own group in a manner analogous to individuals being biased toward themselves.

In one study about the differences between individualistic and collectivistic cultures, a joint team of researchers from Stanford University, the University of Hong Kong, and Hong Kong

University of Science and Technology looked at the differences between the American and Japanese media in their attributions of credit and blame.[21] The researchers examined how the media, specifically the *New York Times* in the U.S. sample and the *Asahi Shimbun* for the Japanese, analyzed "rogue trader" events in both nations—situations where an employee at an investment bank had apparently made independent trading decisions that resulted in huge losses for his employer. The analysis showed that the American newspaper accounts largely focused on the actions of the individual, while the Japanese accounts questioned the organization's systems and control mechanisms. Similarly, when a Japanese athlete wins a sporting event, he or she is more likely to attribute success to fans, family, and coaches than an American athlete would be. One reason for this difference is that East Asian cultures as represented by Japan, China, and Korea come from the tradition of Confucius, which is dominated by social thinking and group loyalty, where each individual derives their identity from their social group. It follows, then, that in a society where the self is defined in collective terms, credit and blame would also be assigned to collectivities rather than to individuals. In Japan, there is a well-known saying: "The nail that sticks up gets hammered down," which conveys the cultural norm that claiming individual credit is actually blameworthy.

The foundational influences on how we take in and dispense credit and blame—including primate and human evolution, early life experience, gender, and national culture—all combine to create lenses from the past through which we view the present. When we go into the office each day, it's easy to forget the heritage that we are bringing with us. However, it's impossible to understand the psychology of the present without taking into account the legacy of our past. Part of my role with clients is to help them look at their situations in a new way, and to consider new strategies for managing credit and blame. One client in particular achieved great success in reframing a highly fraught workplace situation, and then taking a new approach to managing herself and the situation more effectively.

At our first meeting, Dana, an analyst at a large and prestigious hedge fund, expressed her great concern that her boss, Alexandra, would "screw" her on her annual bonus. An Asian American, Dana saw herself as a laid-back West Coaster who had moved to the East Coast after business school, while she described Alexandra as a highly competitive East Coast WASP. Dana felt that her own cultural background, which focused on family, groups, and community, put her at a disadvantage in terms of getting the individual credit she thought she deserved in her Wall Street job. At the same time, she grudgingly admired how easy it was for Alexandra to take credit, and Dana believed that Alexandra's cultural background made it much easier for her to seek out and be comfortable in the spotlight.

However, Dana also described a long list of complaints about Alexandra, including how she took credit for all of Dana's good investment ideas while denying any responsibility for those that didn't do well. As I listened more to the dramatic stories of things Alexandra had done to steal credit, including conveniently rewriting history, I began to wonder about the deeper context for what seemed at first to be a relatively straightforward personality conflict between two highly motivated women. Dana described Alexandra as very insecure in her position, since Alexandra did not have Dana's level of education and experience in the complex derivatives they were trading. In order to demonstrate the value she was adding, Alexandra felt it was necessary to take credit for the ideas of her staff. Although Alexandra was clearly a difficult person and a brutal boss, there were also organizational issues at play here.

I was reminded of Herman Melville's contrasting depiction of the crew and the Native American harpoonists on the *Pequod* in *Moby-Dick*. The crew, including First Mate Starbuck (for whom a large chain of coffee stores was named—the founders actually considered naming the stores Pequod, until one of them realized that the first syllable of that word might have a negative connotation for beverages),[22] had hard-to-evaluate skills and talents, and as a result, depended on Captain Ahab's favorable view of their capabilities for their positions and status on the boat. Meanwhile, the Native American harpoonists, including Queequeg, had skills and talents that were easy to evaluate—they killed the whales. Even Captain Ahab needed to give them some leeway. Melville depicts the crew as being highly circumspect and deferential, while the harpoonists had much more freedom of expression.

Back on dry land, at the hedge fund, Dana said she yearned to have her own "book" so that she could clearly demonstrate her skill in finding and executing big, profitable investments instead of having to spend what she viewed as a burdensome amount of time kissing up to Alexandra. Dana complained that Alexandra had surrounded herself with staff who were not particularly skilled at securities analysis, but who somehow managed to ingratiate themselves. Dana also noted that Alexandra didn't have a clearly defined successor, and she wondered whether this was a deliberate strategy on Alexandra's part to avoid the risk of "replaceability." Finally, Alexandra was described by Dana as paranoid, and as always interposing herself between her staff and anyone else in the organization.

However, Dana also brought her own baggage to work each day. She was aware that some of her interactions with Alexandra reminded her of her own childhood and teenage interactions with her mother. Dana's mother, while very intelligent like her daughter, grew up in a family and culture which emphasized that a woman's place was in the home and so she was pressured to become a homemaker rather than pursue her professional ambitions. Dana's mother was very proud of her daughter and encouraged her to pursue the kind of career that she herself had been unable to. At the same time, she was also envious of Dana and her opportunities. As a result, Dana was ambivalent about her success, uncomfortable receiving too much credit, and would become concerned if she began to sense that she was upstaging her boss.

Alexandra was skilled at identifying insecure staffers and providing praise and reassurance to them before inviting them to work with her. At first, Alexandra provided a motivational "carrot" rather than a motivational "stick." Dana cared very much about getting praised by any boss she worked for, and thought that she would receive praise from Alexandra. Dana complained, though, that the actual experience of working directly for Alexandra was very different from encountering her from afar. This bait and switch was the opposite of what organizational psychologists term *realistic job previews* (*RJPs*). In the short term, an RJP might scare candidates away; but over the long term, research has shown that insofar as realistic previews can help ensure a better fit between an individual and a specific role at a specific organization, RJPs actually increase the likelihood that a candidate will remain satisfied and productive in that role. RJPs and their opposite are ironically alluded to in a famous law students' joke:

A young law student is studying in the law library one day, when suddenly the devil appears. The devil tells the student that if he's willing to sell his soul, the devil will pay off all his law school debts, and promises the student will reap untold delights and rewards. The devil goes so far as to offer to take the student on a safe, round-trip journey to tour hell. The student agrees, and is amazed by the comfort, convenience, and amenities that hell has to offer. There are people lounging at swimming pools, playing golf, tennis, and softball, visiting museums, and going to the theater. They all seem totally serene, fulfilled, and happy. The student agrees to sell his soul and happily pays off his debts.

Unfortunately, when he arrives in hell, it is a totally different place. There is no more golf, tennis, and water sports. Instead, he sees people in excruciating physical and emotional agony, not having eaten, slept, or bathed in days, and interacting with each other in a nasty, brutish, and short manner. The scene looks like a Hieronymus Bosch painting. The young man is horrified and asks the devil, "Why did the preview look so different than this?" The devil replies, "That was the summer associates program."

Alexandra had offered Dana an equivalent of the Faustian summer associates program before they formally started working together, heaping praise on her for her financial analysis and her knack for identifying promising investment opportunities. Dana was just slightly older than the demographic group that the *Wall Street Journal* called The Most Praised Generation, but was as susceptible to being stroked as the Generation Y workers the *Journal* described as needing parental-type validation from their bosses. As we'll see throughout this book, identity, self-esteem, and social esteem are inextricably linked to credit and blame, for better or worse.

Alexandra was known for having two different groups under her supervision. Rather than any formal delineation, these two groups were based on the people Alexandra liked or disliked. Those she liked were frequently rewarded and promoted, while those she didn't like were treated along the spectrum from benign neglect to malignant attention. Organizational psychologists would term this distinction the "in-group" versus the "out-group." For some leaders, their in-groups and out-groups can be quite stable over time, based on similarity or compatibility in terms of work style, personality, values, or other factors. For other leaders, there is not that great a distinction between the two groups. Some leaders manage to treat their whole team as insiders, and some leaders are equal-opportunity persecutors and treat everyone like an outsider. However, for other leaders, like Alexandra, there was a huge distinction between in-group and out-group, and occasional traffic between the two. At times, it seemed that the higher one flew while on Alexandra's good side, the harder one fell when they angered her for any reason. Alexandra was far from consistent or fair in how she treated people.

The political philosopher John Rawls, in his masterwork *A Theory of Justice*, described a criterion for whether a society is just or not, which he called the "veil of ignorance."[23] Basically, the idea is that if you had a choice about which society you would like to live in, and did not know which position you would occupy in that society, you would choose one in which everyone has certain rights and basic resources, rather than one in which a few people capriciously determined laws and in which this small elite unfairly controlled a disproportionate share of the society's resources. The "veil of ignorance" is something worth considering when deciding whether to join a particular organization, or to work for a particular boss. If a boss treats people very differently, it may be best not to assume you will be one of the few lucky ones. If your happiness and fulfillment depend on your being an accredited member of the in-group and not an unappreciated member of the out-group, it may be better to turn down the role and try to find a more just boss or a fairer workplace.

Even as Dana decided to begin reporting to Alexandra, she had had her doubts, and described how she had a difficult time sleeping the night before she made her decision to work for Alexandra. In retrospect, Dana acknowledged, her anxiety about working directly under Alexandra was well founded, and Dana wished she had listened more carefully to her gut. Dana felt that if someone could be obnoxious to anyone, sooner or later they would be obnoxious to everyone. Still, despite her reservations, Dana agreed to work for her.

At first, things proceeded well for Dana, who worked hard and produced insightful analysis and good recommendations. Alexandra conveyed appreciation, and asked Dana to take on additional work in a broader market area. But within short order, what had started out smooth became toxic and rocky. Dana had recommended that the firm take a position in a certain kind of security, and Alexandra was reluctant to do so because it was a complex instrument, and one that she didn't fully understand. Dana convinced her, though, staying late into the night to create PowerPoint decks describing the attributes of the investment, as well as outlining what its value would be under different scenarios. Alexandra agreed to recommend the securities purchase to the firm's investment committee.

Dana described the scene at the investment committee meeting as being straight out of *Working Girl*, in which the evil boss, played by Sigourney Weaver, tries to steal credit for the idea of the ambitious secretary, played by Melanie Griffith. Alexandra claimed that the idea was hers, and she described having directed Dana to do the very analysis that Dana had proposed and done on her own initiative in order to educate Alexandra about the proposed trade. Dana watched with shock as Alexandra first took full credit for her new idea, and then described how responsible Dana had been for suggesting another investment idea—one that had gone terribly wrong and that had actually been Alexandra's idea. Dana kept her composure, but she told me later she felt like she had been transported to the world of *The Twilight Zone* or Orwell's *1984*. From all of Dana's accounts, Alexandra had a "totalitarian" leadership style, and had come to believe in her own propaganda, so the latter analogy seemed on target.

Alexandra's behavior struck me as being somewhere between the late trading mutual fund scandals of a few years ago, in which trades were made after trading hours, and the scam in *The Sting*, in which bets are placed on horse races after they have already been run. Instead of taking actual risks, the mutual fund traders, the scammers—and Alexandra—would reap the benefits of betting on events after they occurred. A better run, less political organization would not have tolerated the kind of methods that Alexandra employed in order to swoop in at the last minute to get credit for good investments, or to disclaim blame when transactions went bad. The organization would have also benefited if Alexandra had to choose between a staff role analogous to Melville's Starbuck, or an investing role analogous to Queequeg's. Her ability to retroactively change her position after the investment tides had turned was to her benefit but directly contrary to the organization's.

Dana sought out coaching for a practical reason—she wanted to make sure she was taking any steps necessary to ensure her bonus would fairly reflect her contributions. Alexandra was stealing credit for her ideas, and Dana was concerned that she would be vulnerable to Alexandra's whims when bonus time came around. As we worked together, Dana and I explored different possible strategies, ranging from confronting Alexandra in private to trying to reach out to other senior leaders in the firm in order to more clearly establish Dana's role in identifying profitable investments. There were risks for Dana in each of these strategies, and there was also a risk in doing nothing. If Dana had decided to wage a political battle to get credit for her investment ideas, she might have won the battle but lost the war. I endeavored to help her reframe the situation from a negative one in which she was helpless into a more positive one in which she would benefit in a variety of ways. After all, she was working for a prestigious organization, making a very good salary even independent of her potential bonus, and learning a lot about the markets in general and certain exotic financial instruments in particular.

I also encouraged her to think about credit and blame as a kind of currency that she could trade with Alexandra at a favorable exchange rate. Recalling a Japanese movie, *A Taxing Woman* (1987), in which an organized crime syndicate buys a winning lottery ticket for more than its face value because it will help it launder money, I suggested that Dana consider whether credit for good investment ideas might actually be worth more to Alexandra than to Dana, since Alexandra had to justify her high compensation to the company.

As tempting as it can be in the workplace to insist on fairness, people often make the mistake of suboptimizing their political or financial position because of self-esteem concerns, as my friend Pria nearly did. In *The Devil Wears Prada*, Anne Hathaway's character triumphs in her career by not internalizing the criticism of her boss, brilliantly portrayed by Meryl Streep. Instead, she bets that working for the Devil will pay off in her later career—a strategy that is validated at the end of the story. As in the movie, Dana's story also had a happy ending. Dana learned to manage her frustration, disable the buttons that Alexandra was pushing, and focus on her job. Sometimes the best strategy is to wait for the organization's internal "credit market" to right itself over time, especially if someone is being radically overvalued, as Alexandra had been, or highly undervalued, as Dana had been. Alexandra ended up getting fired when the firm finally realized she wasn't worth the money she was making. And Dana got to run her own investments, now receiving full credit for her frequent good ideas, and being held accountable in a fair way for her rare bad ones.

Dana's story helps illustrate the complexity involved in the relationships we have with others in the workplace, whether they be co-workers or our boss. Just as in our personal relationships, it can be easy for us to fall into the trap of blaming everyone else for our troubles rather than working to understand how our own personality traits, decisions, and behaviors impact those relationships. When we challenge ourselves to take a more nuanced view of those we have working relationships with, we can actually achieve better outcomes. I never met Alexandra, but I was able to assist Dana with developing and executing a successful strategy for managing their relationship. In our work together I helped Dana gain a better understanding of her own personality, Alexandra's personality, and the interpersonal chemistry between the two of them.

CHAPTER 3

Typecasting Blame

In addition to the evolutionary and family influences that help determine how people assign and react to credit and blame, differences in personality also play a significant role in the blame game. When it comes to understanding our workplaces, and the challenges and opportunities we face when we come to work each day, others' personalities matter, our personality matters, and the complex interaction between theirs and our own also matters. We've all encountered people who seem to always take credit when things go well and blame others when they don't, and/or people who never share any credit or accept any blame. In rarer cases, we might have come across people who seem to always blame themselves, or who struggle to take credit for anything.

It is often true that those with whom we are having the worst issues in this regard have extreme personalities in one way or another—something we'll take a close look at in this chapter. We'll explore how established personality dimensions and types are particularly prone to certain reactions or problems in the realm of credit and blame. But before getting into that, it's important to consider several caveats. Just designating someone as a blaming type, or a credit hog, isn't going to get us very far in learning how to cope with the daily challenges that person presents us with. In evaluating how a specific problem may be due to a particular person's basic personality—the person with whom this comes into play most often being, of course, our boss—it is essential that we not think in black-and-white terms. This is true not only because doing so leads to simplification that isn't helpful in understanding the problem, but because we may then react in simplistic and impulsive ways that only serve to make things worse. If we convey to others "either you're with me or against me," they may be inclined to choose "against" simply because they resent being forced to make such a stark and simplistic choice.

One of my most important roles as an executive coach and organizational psychologist is to challenge people to think more broadly about the individual, relational, team, cultural, structural, economic, demographic, generational, and even historical reasons why people behave a certain way. To simply credit or blame an individual's personality for performance or behavior without considering the broader context can be to commit the *personality attribution error,* focusing too narrowly on specific personality traits rather than general character or the situational constraints a person is coping with.

Essentially, we live in a gray movie that we instead see as a black-and-white snapshot. We observe a boss misassigning credit and blame to herself and us, and it's tempting to attribute that behavior simply to her personality and to imagine she has always been that way, and will always be that way. But this may lead us to discount a host of other factors that are almost surely at play, including not only the situation that our boss faces, which we likely have only a partial picture of, but also our own subjective perceptions and resulting behaviors.

Even when considering personality on its own, we will be much better off if we come to understand that there are a number of underlying personality characteristics—or "traits"—that may not only account for why some people seem to be so particularly difficult to deal with, but also make them unaware of how unfair and counterproductive their behavior is. After all, if they were aware of the strange, irrational, unfair, and ultimately self-defeating ways in which they are handing out and responding to credit and blame, would they still be doing so?

In discussing personality types, therefore, it's critical to keep in mind that any general set of attributes is by definition an oversimplification of the true complexity of a specific individual's personality. Personality remains one of the greatest mysteries in psychology, and even experts can disagree about the meaning and importance of a general type, say, that of the "introvert." Introversion and extroversion are tendencies that exist on a spectrum, and can vary according to time, place, and situation. People are often surprised when they change roles, for example, switching from research and development to sales, that making the transition from introvert to extrovert is much easier than they thought it would be. Therefore, while it's tempting to think that someone is just a "blamer," the real picture is inevitably much more complex. A "blamer" today may become a "crediter" tomorrow.

In her thoughtful and well-researched book *The Cult of Personality: How Personality Tests Are Leading Us to Miseducate Our Children, Mismanage Our Companies, and Misunderstand Ourselves*, Annie Murphy Paul goes into great detail about both the prevalence and the limitations of personality tests.[1] Many people who take these tests get different results each time they take them, and the tests' prediction of behavior in the workplace is tenuous at best. Paul's point is that personality tests often reflect more about the worldviews and biases of the people who develop and administer them than about the people who, willingly or reluctantly, take them.

Paul mentions psychologist Dan McAdam's idea of "The Psychology of the Stranger,"[2] which basically states that we can know someone's personality type, and yet not really know that person in a meaningful way. Paul advocates paying closer attention to a person's "story" in order to get to know them better, rather than pigeonholing him or her as a certain type. In my consulting work, I have found that there is much wisdom in Paul's recommendation. When trying to understand why someone is a chronic blamer, it can be much more helpful to know that he grew up in the shadow of a more successful older sister than to identify any particular element of his personality, or to know his personality type.

One of the great debates in psychology, in fact, concerns whether the person or the situation is more important in determining behavior, which is similar to the recurring debate about whether nature or nurture is more important in how a person develops as they mature. The answer, clearly, is that genetics, physiology, temperament, environment, experience, and situations all play important roles not only in what people do or don't do, but also in the way they assign credit and blame to themselves and others, as well as in how they perceive or react to the credit and blame they receive from others. When considering how to deal with these issues with any given person, or in any given situation, it is crucial to keep complexity foremost in mind.

So, although it's important to consider that personality issues may be at play, we also need to think about the larger context and how that might be affecting the problem. Stress and anxiety can cause people's bad tendencies to flare up, or even cause those who don't normally exhibit certain temperaments or personality traits to behave as though they do. An example might be a co-worker or boss who is having some kind of serious difficulty in her personal life, which causes her a great deal of distress. This person, whom you always thought of as calm and reasonable, now suddenly erupts at the slightest mistake, blaming everyone around her, which makes for a miserable work environment. Or perhaps you have a colleague who is reasonable and pleasant until he feels threatened, and then he seems to transform from Dr. Jekyll into Mr. Hyde. There is a phenomenon that psychologists have termed *threat-rigidity*, in which people who are threatened become rigid in their thinking and behavior. In the workplace, this rigidity can become highly contagious—and highly problematic. When people perceive that they have been unfairly blamed or deprived of credit, they may begin to think and act in a more angry and inflexible manner, thereby threatening others in a chain reaction.

In fact, what may seem to us to be "traits" may actually be the symptoms of people in an unfortunate "state." This may be due to elevated levels of stress hormones, like cortisol, or to a psycho-physiological state that Daniel Goleman termed an "amygdala hijack," when a person loses his or her emotional equilibrium and control.[3] On the other side of the spectrum, researchers at the University of Rostock in Germany investigating possible hormonal treatments for autism have found that increasing levels of oxytocin, sometimes known as "the cuddle hormone" (which is intimately involved in mammalian bonding), can increase empathy,[4] and people who are more empathic are less likely to reflexively blame. In addition to cuddling and sex, drugs also can increase empathy. A recent *New York Times* article described how people taking psilocybin, the active ingredient in "magic mushrooms," reported having greater empathy for others, even their ex-spouses. Other drugs like Ecstasy (also known as MDMA) have been shown to temporarily reduce fear, anger, and aggression.[5] Alexander "Sasha" Theodore Shulgin, who is credited with having popularized Ecstasy, said, "The drug should have been called 'empathy' for what it did, but I believe they felt that 'empathy' didn't have the same sensational ring to it. So they called it 'Ecstasy,' which is a strange name but it stuck."[6]

Of course, while this is helpful information, it's unlikely that your organization's employee policies would allow you to directly increase your boss's level of oxytocin. The important point is to be aware that in many situations, the states brought on by physiological reactions and/or social influences can minimize individual differences in personality. In certain circumstances, people with different personalities find themselves not only acting in similar ways but also crediting or blaming others in similar ways. In a toxic corporate culture, for example, everyone might get swept up into contagious finger-pointing, while in a stronger, team-based culture, everyone might be predisposed to share credit with teammates. The lines between what someone does, and who someone is, can be thinly drawn.

This is why, in the chapters that follow, we'll examine a number of common situational factors and social pressures that cause problems at work. But with all of the aforementioned caveats about the complexity and unpredictability of personality, as well as the dynamic interaction between "person" and "situation," in this chapter we'll look at the role of personality.

Let's start by examining a well-established model of five basic building blocks of "normal" personality that is widely used in psychology. Then we'll look at a taxonomy of personality types that are more extreme and challenging. Knowing about these types can be helpful because they provide a fairly good description of how people will deal with credit and blame in harmful and hurtful ways. In reading about these types, you may well recognize your boss, or certain colleagues you are experiencing issues with. These types are meant to serve as frameworks for observing and understanding patterns of behavior; but they are more useful in providing questions about *how* your boss and colleagues may be acting than in providing answers as to *why* they are doing so.

There are four key considerations, though, when thinking about these types. The first is that each of us has the potential to exhibit several different patterns of behavior. Second, the way someone acts and reacts in a given workplace situation will be due not only to his or her personality but also to specific interactions with others—as we'll explore in the next chapter, people who work together can bring out the worst, or the best, in each other. Third, these characteristics are nested in the larger context of who a person is. Two people could have the exact same personality profile, and still be very different in how they act in general, and handle credit and blame in particular, due to gender, culture, education, socioeconomic status, and so on. And finally, situational factors interact with all personality dimensions and general personality types to influence behavior.

The true value, then, of knowing about these categories is not in coming up with "profiles" to determine how you should deal with difficult people; general categories or types of personality will never have sufficient explanatory or predictive power for that purpose. The value, rather, is in helping us to step back from the heat of the moment and to know that the person we're having trouble with is probably treating others that way, too. Issues of credit and blame are more painful when we take them personally; the more we learn about other people's difficulties and issues, the less personally we can take some of what they throw our way, and this perspective can be highly liberating.

Even in a situation where you are indisputably being treated unfairly, it's still important to take a step back before deciding if and how to act. As we saw in the last chapter, the ways in which we react to credit and blame can quickly become more problematic than the original issue for which we felt undercredited or overblamed. It can be highly unproductive and unpleasant for individuals, teams, and entire organizations when people take on a retaliatory mind-set in the face of real or perceived "disses." What might seem fair and strategic in the moment can often appear unhelpful and ill-considered when looked back upon.

Even when faced with clear and convincing evidence that the apportionment of credit and blame are unfair and have been woefully out of alignment with reality, in all but the rarest situations, a slower and more mindful approach is better than a faster, more reactive one.

So, even if you do recognize your boss or a colleague in these descriptions of personality types, it's important to remember that one person's toxic boss can be another's merely annoying micromanager. Toxicity is a subjective judgment in the eye of the beholder, and depends on both intrapersonal and interpersonal chemistry.

THE BIG FIVE

Although personality tests like the Myers-Briggs Type Indicator (MBTI) are better known, "the Big Five" personality model is the most well established and research-based model of human personality, and draws upon decades of empirical and statistical research.[7] A data analysis technique known as *factor analysis* was used to cull through hundreds of trait descriptors, and the analysis determined that most of the variance in human personality can be accounted for by these five dimensions. Although many researchers have contributed over the course of several decades, Paul Costa and Robert McCrae at the National Institutes of Health are often credited with having popularized and codified the Big Five.

The five categories—whose first letters, depending on how they are ordered, comprise the acronyms OCEAN or CANOE—are:

- Openness (to experience): High scores indicate an inventive and curious nature; low scores indicate caution and conservatism

- Conscientiousness: High scorers tend to be efficient and organized; low scorers are easygoing and careless
- Extroversion: People high on this dimension are outgoing and energetic; those who rate low are shy and socially withdrawn
- Agreeableness: High scores indicate a friendly and compassionate person; low scores indicate that people are competitive and outspoken
- Neuroticism: High scorers are more sensitive and nervous; low scorers tend to be secure and confident

Within each of these Big Five dimensions are six "subfactors" which further differentiate individuals:

Openness to Experience	imagination
	artistic interests
	emotionality
	adventurousness
	intellect
	liberalism
Conscientiousness	self-efficacy
	orderliness
	dutifulness
	achievement-striving
	self-discipline
	cautiousness
Extroversion	friendliness
	gregariousness
	assertiveness
	activity level
	excitement-seeking
	cheerfulness

Agreeableness	trust
	morality
	altruism
	cooperation
	modesty
	sympathy
Neuroticism	anxiety
	anger
	depression
	self-consciousness
	immoderation
	vulnerability

It's important to mention that just because these subfactors are associated with the main traits doesn't mean that everyone who scores high on Conscientiousness, for example, will score high on all of the subfactors associated with it. Even if someone scores high on *dutifulness*, it doesn't necessarily mean that she will also score high on *achievement-striving*, which is another subfactor of Conscientiousness. While both traits correlate with one another strongly enough to be subfactors of Conscientiousness, they are also somewhat independent of one another.

The particular combination of traits and subtraits that characterize an individual can help describe how that person approaches credit and blame. For example, a person who scores high on the Agreeableness trait and also high on that trait's subfactor of *modesty*—defined as "high scorers on this scale do not like to claim that they are better than other people"—may have a good deal of trouble in claiming credit that they are due. But another person who is high on Agreeableness but low on *modesty* may not have that problem at all. And that same person who is high on *modesty* might be low on the *altruism* subfactor of

Agreeableness, which measures the extent to which someone is motivated to be helpful and generous to others, for example, in sharing credit for achievements. So, although that person might not be a credit-grabber, she might also not be especially generous, or altruistic, in assigning credit to others.

A highly introverted person—someone scoring low on the Extroversion trait—who also scores low on the subfactor of *assertiveness* is another type who might find it very hard to claim credit. But an introverted person who is high on *assertiveness* may be better at finding ways to get his due credit, just not in a public way.

Someone who is high on Conscientiousness and the subfactor of *dutifulness*, which is the extent to which a person is guided by a sense of duty and moral obligation, might be likely to accept more blame than is really appropriate if he feels like he hasn't lived up to his own standards. Someone who is high on the Neuroticism dimension would likely blame themselves more than others would, and, particularly if he or she also scored high on the *vulnerability* subfactor of Neuroticism, would likely become acutely distressed if blamed by others, since *vulnerability* measures the extent to which people are given to losing composure in the face of pressure or stress. Someone who in addition to scoring high on *vulnerability* also scores high on the *anger* subfactor of Neuroticism, which captures the extent to which people are likely to feel bitter or angry when things don't go their way, is likely to express that distress in the form of angrily blaming others, and to feel cheated, if they do not believe they are getting their due.

The Big Five dimensions and subfactors can also help illuminate how different individuals either work together harmoniously or tend to come into conflict with one another. It's easy to see how low scorers and high scorers in a particular trait could find themselves at odds when it comes to credit and blame. A high scorer on Conscientiousness, for instance, might find it easy to find fault with a low-scoring co-worker who is consistently late in filing reports. People who scored high on Openness to Experience might find it hard to work with people who are not willing to reconsider how they have assigned credit or blame to themselves or others. A person who is highly *dutiful* would likely have a hard time working with someone who does not hold him- or herself to high standards, even though that other person might be quite high on *achievement-striving*, and both of them may be high in overall Conscientiousness.

Introverts and extroverts can also have problems relating to, and working with, each other. The challenge is that introverts, who tend to be reserved, speak softly, and enjoy working alone, often find themselves competing for credit with extroverts, who are more inclined to be "out there" promoting their ideas and themselves. Since introverts are less comfortable with self-promotion, it can be challenging for them to find ways to collect their due credit without compromising who they are. As Nancy Ancowitz, author of *Self-Promotion for Introverts*, writes: "Gaining visibility is a big challenge for introverts. We often immerse ourselves in our tasks, plunge the depths of our inner worlds, and neglect to come up for air to take credit."[8]

The helpful strategy for introverts, then, is to push themselves to do new things, such as—as Ancowitz suggests—writing follow-up emails after meetings to confirm and acknowledge key points, or beginning to host or even speak at meetings and conferences. In general, being aware of how one's personality can present challenges and opportunities is very helpful, since that knowledge enables people to create strategies that build on their strengths and minimize the negative impact of areas for development.

The Big Five personality dimensions can be functional or dysfunctional, depending on the person and the situation. These attributes can be thought of as analogous to the "molecules" of personality. Just as water can change phase from ice to water and to steam, the way personality traits influence behavior and interact with one another can also change over time. In some situations, the same personality attribute can be more like ice, water, or steam, rendering it difficult to differentiate between "trait" and "state." Sometimes, in other words, it's hard to tell whether your boss has always been an ice queen or has just recently been frozen by a cold workplace atmosphere.

To try to describe all the combinations of dimensions that might account for people's behavior regarding credit and blame would be impossible. As mentioned earlier, the point of introducing this framework is not to suggest that you can or should use it to come up with an exact diagnosis of your boss and colleagues— or of yourself. But I hope that this introduction helps show how complex personality issues influence how people deal with credit and blame, and also that the combination of personalities in any given situation can play a big role in how things unfold.[9]

These five major personality dimensions are widely considered by the academic and professional community of psychologists to be the basic characteristics of so-called "normal" personality. Another typology that has been well established in the field, which also greatly illuminates dynamics of credit and blame, is that of what are considered to be a set of "dysfunctional" personality types.

HOGAN'S ANTIHEROES

Personality can be thought of as "a culture of one," meaning that it is a way of looking at the world, and a way of acting in the world, that an individual develops to adapt to his or her environment. When functional and adaptive, an individual's personality successfully balances internal drives and societal demands.

However, what is functional and adaptive in one situation—for example, in one's early life in a family environment—may not always work for an adult in the workplace. Even there, the strategies people use to protect their self-esteem, their sense of identity, and their social standing may also be functional in the short term but highly problematic over the longer term.

Psychologists have described three maladaptive personality categories (*maladaptive* here meaning the "costs" of that particular pattern of traits and attributes outweigh the "benefits"). Although they apply to both credit and blame, these three categories are defined in a way more closely related to blame. The three are *extrapunitive*—people who excessively blame others; *impunitive*—people who deny blame to an extreme extent; and *intropunitive*—people who blame themselves too harshly.

These three categories were further differentiated into eleven personality types by the renowned psychologists Robert and Joyce Hogan in the 1990s in the *Hogan Development Survey*, which they created and validated at their company, the eponymous Hogan Assessment Systems.[10] This well-established research-based taxonomy of types is the most helpful benchmark for assessing how people assign credit and blame to themselves and others, and how they react to the credit and blame they receive from others. In the next section, I'll introduce the eleven types and describe how they can be placed into the three categories just mentioned.[11]

But before doing so, I want to emphasize that it is important to realize that if people are behaving in these ways, coping with their behavior is likely not a simple matter of figuring out how to get them to change their ways. Their wacky perceptions and personal reality may be so deeply ingrained that attempts to present contrary "evidence," or to argue that they should assign credit and blame in a different way, will be counterproductive. Challenges to their worldview may only serve to make them feel threatened and even more defensive. So, after introducing the types, I'll discuss ways in which you can try to contend with the challenges of working with these kinds of people by taking a more subtle and patient approach.[12]

EXTRAPUNITIVE

When it comes to taking responsibility, an extrapunitive person looks anywhere but at themselves, consistently blaming their mistakes on other people or on external situations. Their colleagues and co-workers are likely to be frequent recipients of unwarranted blame.

An executive coaching client of mine, whom I'll call Genna, sought advice about how to manage her very talented but perennially angry boss. William was the founder of a successful investment firm, and Genna was his director of administration. Genna was less concerned about William's anger toward her than about the way he constantly berated the junior investment professionals at the firm. Always blaming others, and never taking any personal responsibility, William was extra-extrapunitive. Genna found herself in the role of "den mother" at the firm as people came to seek her support after being excoriated by William. She noted how William's outbursts negatively impacted the organization, causing people to feel insecure and walk on eggshells around him. William harshly blamed all of the people some of the time, and some of the people all of the time. As a result, there was high turnover, with talented people leaving for greener pastures as soon as other opportunities presented themselves.

William was a frequent assigner of blame and complained that many of the members of his staff "didn't get it." He blamed them for not doing what he felt they were supposed to do, when they were supposed to do it. Something of a workaholic, William was constantly busy and inaccessible to his staff, preferring meetings with investors to managing his team. People working under him began to dread their interactions with him since they experienced a "damned if you do, damned if you don't" paradox. If they approached William to ask him for instructions and guidance, he would snap at them that they needed to figure things out themselves. And if they didn't approach him and misunderstood his goals and expectations, he would blame them for doing the wrong thing.

Although Genna was tempted to explicitly confront William and let him know how stressed and upset the investment professionals were feeling, I coached her to take a more subtle approach. Together, Genna and I looked back at the situations where William had been disappointed and angry, and saw that there were common themes, often involving how investors and investments were classified. In fact, sometimes it was hard to put an investment into any preexisting category, and at other times an investment could be placed into several categories. Drawing on her emotional intelligence, Genna realized that neither challenging William's tendency to blame nor trying to defend the staff would work. Doing either would have just made William more angry and less able to reflect. Instead, Genna simply communicated the staff's questions to William at opportune moments. When he was calm and had time to focus, she would casually say, "I think the team is unsure about how to classify investment X." Sometimes he would react impulsively and say, "That should be clear to them," and Genna would back off instead of pushing him.

Genna was persistent, though, and over time, William came to see that the staff were not to blame for their confusion in classifying investments. Genna suggested they create a task force to come up with recommendations for clearer guidelines, and William agreed this would be helpful. The task force presented a few alternative approaches, William picked one, and as a result there was much less confusion. Genna's patient approach had helped protect William from himself, circumventing his tendency to blame his staff, and helping both William and the organization to solve the underlying systemic problem.

EXTRAPUNITIVE SUBTYPES

Excitable — or Volatile Guardian

Excitable types have mercurial and moody management styles and, as a result, are likely to make hasty decisions and assign blame inappropriately. Because they are so volatile, they assign credit and blame based on mood, not facts, and it's very hard to figure out how to either please them or avoid their wrath. This is one "type" where it's particularly hard to get a read on what their "traits" are because their "states" are so changeable. They can quickly move from giving staff too much credit to blaming them excessively and becoming quite disagreeable without warning. Staffers come to realize that they shouldn't get too close to an excitable boss, since the higher you fly, the harder and faster you can fall. Excitable bosses exemplify the "can dish it out but can't take it" pattern of blame. Given negative feedback or blamed by others, they can become highly defensive, may lose their temper or composure, and may take even well-intentioned feedback as critical, hurtful, and unfair. The financial services executive who hung up on his subordinate had some of the attributes of the excitable type, as he initially lost his cool when blamed by the human resources department and became defensive thereafter. This kind of boss often frightens and demoralizes staff, who may become insecure and withdrawn. Their staff might also be so focused on the boss's volatile moods and priorities that they lose track of the tasks at hand and make avoidable mistakes.

Cautious—or Sensitive Retirer

Cautious types have a hands-off management style, to the point of indecisiveness, and make decisions intended to minimize the risk of being blamed. Difficult or even impossible to communicate with, or even reach on the phone or via email, they avoid the spotlight, declining invitations to receive public recognition, and withdraw even more than usual after being blamed. They tend to be pessimistic, and to expect that their efforts will lead to blame rather than credit. Hypersensitive to being blamed, such cautious types are too defensive or anxious to learn from feedback, and can be particularly exasperating as colleagues. As managers, they are fearful of giving too much credit to their team, and may want their staff to avoid the spotlight too. This kind of leader often leaves his or her team feeling neglected or abandoned, which may be demoralizing and demotivating. The cautious leader can also cause bottlenecks, where work piles up and raises staff anxiety that they will be blamed for missed deadlines, or for delivering lower quality work because of compressed timelines. If anyone questions the cautious person on any of these dynamics, he or she may withdraw even further.

Skeptical—or Wary Watcher

Skeptical types have a fight-or-flight management style, and lead their teams either to take a belligerent stance or to withdraw from projects at the slightest hint that things may go wrong. This type of person believes that others will unfairly blame or discredit him, and doubts the sincerity of the people who give credit. Because these types are apprehensive about credit and blame offered by others, they make decisions intended to limit their vulnerability. They are unwilling to take any risks whatsoever, or to experiment with new approaches, since doing so creates the potential for blame. Since they project their own weaknesses on others, they tend to blame others for their own problems and shortcomings, and to imagine that others are blaming them. For example, if a skeptical person blames a teammate for a project delay, they may perceive that their teammate is blaming *them*. They may also perceive they are being criticized or blamed even when others are simply offering constructive advice. Because of this lack of openness and "fight-or-flight" approach, their teams also tend to become wary of others across the organization and have a hard time with collaboration.

Leisurely—or Rationalizing Blamer

Leisurely people work at their own pace and according to their own preferences, ignoring others' requests. If things go wrong, they refuse to take responsibility, usually blaming whoever assigned the challenging task to them instead of acknowledging their role in whatever did or did not happen. They appear envious of others who get more credit, are constantly alert for signs of not being sufficiently appreciated, and come to believe that they always get a raw deal in terms of being undercredited and overblamed. As bosses and colleagues, leisurely types are competitive and unreliable, but their hostility may be hard to detect at first because they seem friendly and collaborative on the surface. The leisurely type may be even more challenging for superiors than for subordinates, as they tend not to follow orders and to overpromise and underdeliver.

IMPUNITIVE

When it comes to taking responsibility, an impunitive person will spin facts and refuse to acknowledge that mistakes have been made. People who work with or for them, or who supervise them, are likely to become exasperated by the high level of vagueness and denial that impunitive people demonstrate.

I once coached the CEO of a large health care nonprofit that was in the midst of tough challenges and major changes. The CEO, Robert, described to me how major sources of funding were being cut back, and how the organization needed to reduce costs, make its existing processes more efficient, and change a lackadaisical culture into a high-performance one. He was seeking coaching as he led the change efforts, and wanted to make sure he was aligning his team to achieve a series of ambitious goals. At an offsite meeting that I helped facilitate, his senior management team discussed the organization's strengths, weaknesses, opportunities, and threats, and then created small working teams. Each team was tasked with achieving specific goals over the following six months, at which time the entire team would reconvene at another offsite meeting to benchmark progress.

The chief administrative officer, Don, was known for holding others—but not himself—accountable to specific quantitative metrics. Despite his skepticism about Don, Robert put him in charge of a working team that had been tasked with putting new processes into place to improve operational efficiency. Robert knew that the progress of Don and his team would be hard to pin down, but he thought that the working structure would ensure that they would have the same kind of goals and accountabilities as all the other working teams.

In advance of the second offsite meeting, Robert and Don

met to discuss Don's team's progress. At this meeting, Don shared with Robert a preview of a PowerPoint deck titled "Metrics." Robert's first reaction on seeing the presentation was relief, thinking that despite Don's tendency to obfuscate, he had in fact done what he was supposed to do and created for his team the same kind of "report card" that he was well known for using to benchmark others' progress. As Don went through the presentation, though, Robert's relief turned to surprise and then anger when it became clear that the "metrics" being presented were all focused on what had been tried rather than what had been achieved. Don had listed statistics such as "my working team has begun to implement 83 percent of the new processes we agreed to." What Robert had expected, and every other team leader had presented, was not statistics about effort but statistics about outcomes. Don had conveniently reinterpreted his team's task to avoid blame for their lack of progress. As Robert later told me, "Just because they 'tried' it doesn't mean they 'did' it."

However, despite Robert's anger and disappointment, Don remained unconcerned about his team's performance. Robert's lesson was that as the leader of the organization, he had to do more upfront work to establish clearer accountabilities, so that Don and everyone else would be measured against results, instead of being able to deny blame by changing the rules in the middle of the game. Robert made clear to Don that his performance going forward would be measured by outcomes, not efforts, and he let Don know that the "metrics" in the future would be established by Robert, not Don. Don finally got the message that he could no longer be impunitive with impunity. By bringing Don into line, Robert ensured that the culture change he was pushing for actually occurred.

IMPUNITIVE SUBTYPES

Bold—or Big Person on Campus

Bold types lead with the main purpose of receiving personal credit or glory. They require a substantial amount of praise, feel they deserve it much more than others, and constantly talk about their achievements or talents. When things go wrong or they make mistakes, they deny or distort information and "rewrite history" in order to avoid getting blamed. Even if they have made errors, they become disproportionately hurt when blamed since they believe that they deserve credit for simply being who they are, regardless of their actual contributions or achievements. Bold types "kiss up and kick down," strategically ingratiating with their superiors in order to avoid blame, while neglecting to give their staffs any credit for their ideas or contributions. This dysfunctional pattern also causes people to assign credit and blame to others based on bias, shared similarities, and favoritism, rather than on merit, and to believe some people deserve only credit while others deserve only blame.

Alexandra fit the bold profile quite well, which is what made it so challenging for Dana to work for her. As we'll discuss further in chapter 6, Jim Collins describes the most effective and successful "Level 5 leaders" in his bestseller, *Good to Great*, as being exactly the opposite of bold types.[13] When it comes to credit and blame, Collins writes that these exemplary leaders "look in the mirror" when things go wrong and take the blame themselves; and they "look out the window" when success is achieved, sharing the credit with others.

Mischievous — or High Wire Walker

Mischievous types cut corners and bend rules in order to achieve their goals, and do whatever they believe is necessary to get the credit they think they deserve. They can be so envious that they claim credit that is rightfully due to others. In addition to what they see as their due, they also want to be credited for taking bold risks and demonstrating courage. When things go wrong, this personality type is skilled at avoiding blame or responsibility. Mischievous types are highly untrustworthy. The risk to their teams is that others in the organization will associate staffers with their reckless and slippery boss and come to distrust them as well.

Reserved — or Indifferent Daydreamer

Reserved people tend to take a purely task-based and technical approach to leadership, ignoring the human side of the equation. They seem not to get the importance of credit or blame for themselves or others, and will deny blame if it is assigned to them. They do not demonstrate any concern or anxiety about whether or not they or their teams are credited or blamed, and fail to congratulate other people on their accomplishments. Because they are so "checked out," they tend to ignore feedback from others, and do not provide potentially helpful feedback to their own staff. As a result, their teams tend to lack a sense of cohesion or commitment.

Colorful—or Thespian

Colorful types are focused on getting attention and creating buzz about themselves, and resent anyone who does not pay attention to their successes. Highly extroverted, they want to be noticed by everyone they come into contact with, and they quickly become demotivated and bored if public credit is not forthcoming. These people crave attention so much that, given the choice, they would choose blame and attention over not being noticed. They also become uncomfortable when others receive recognition, and may try to upstage those who are working with or for them. As a result, they can be hard to work with either one-on-one or on a team since they draw so much attention to themselves, often depriving others of their due. They will only share credit with others as a means of winning them over and can quickly cycle between overcrediting and over-blaming other people. When things go wrong, they refuse to acknowledge that they have made mistakes, and may become quite dramatic when blamed. They expect people to see them as charming, and never to blame them for anything.

Imaginative—or Assertive Daydreamer

Imaginative types manage in an odd or eccentric manner, and seem to credit or blame others based on superstition or magical thinking rather than the facts on hand. They provide confusing rationales for why they make mistakes and are hard to "pin down" about their role in achieving poor results. They appear anxious about the abstract possibility of being blamed in the future, but are indifferent when actually blamed by other people. It can be hard to relate to this kind of boss or colleague, because they seem so indifferent to the very things that others care about so much.

INTROPUNITIVE

People who direct blame inward, often to an extreme extent, are called intropunitive. Although it is much more common for individuals to be self-serving and blame others or deny blame, excessive self-blame can also be problematic. Women are more likely than men to be intropunitive, and this tendency, as mentioned earlier, may relate to the higher incidence of depression among women than men.

One of my coaching clients had been a top scientist in a prestigious, mid-sized pharmaceutical company. Katerina had twenty-five years of experience and had won all kinds of professional recognition both in the United States and abroad. She was extremely loyal to her boss, the CEO, and mainly focused on receiving recognition from him. Then her company was acquired by another company, and her boss was forced out. For political reasons, the top science job went to her counterpart at the second, bigger pharmaceutical company. Even though Katerina received an offer to stay and report to her counterpart, she decided to seek employment elsewhere. She blamed herself for focusing too much on her research and her former boss, and for not having played the political game or networked with senior executives of the acquiring company, thereby ceding control to her counterpart, whom she soon came to see as a rival.

After discussing her career goals and preferences, she and I scheduled a practice interview. As the interviewer, I asked her about her past experience, key accomplishments, and career motivators. Katerina was confident and relaxed, demonstrating mastery of her field and giving the impression of exactly the kind of person a CEO would want running the science at a biotech or pharmaceutical company of any size. Then, I asked her, "Why did you leave your last employer?" and, like many other clients and candidates I've helped with practice interviews, she totally froze up.

Instead of the poised and charismatic person I'd been speaking with just a few minutes earlier, Katerina suddenly seemed like a teenager who had gotten into a fender bender while taking her parents' car out for a joyride. She stopped making eye contact, muttered some short, rehearsed-sounding platitudes like, "I wasn't very good at managing the politics," and, "When the CEO left, I was on my own," and seemed to literally shrink back in her chair. She conveyed all the sincerity of a hostage making a statement on television praising how well she had been treated by her captors. It was as if a switch had been flicked and suddenly the last twenty-five years of her career had been one big failure. I shared these observations with her and asked her how she was feeling. She readily acknowledged that she hated talking about the circumstances of her departure, which, although it had occurred several months earlier, were still very emotional for her.

Over our next few meetings, we practiced answers to this question until she no longer cringed. Through coaching and feedback, she began to gain comfort in answering in a thoughtful and balanced way. Instead of a rehearsed, quick answer, each time we conducted this practice exercise she would use different words to describe her perspective on what had happened, and why. It was very clear as we practiced that she was listening to herself tell the story, and considering new ways of looking at things every time she recounted the events. She stopped giving the impression of an apologetic self-blaming teenager, and instead was able to continue coming across as the competent and accomplished scientist that she was. When Katerina's actual interviews came around, she was so well prepared to answer the dreaded "Why did you leave your last employer?" question that she no longer feared it.

I was very glad when she called to tell me that she had accepted a lucrative offer to be the top scientist in another organization.

INTROPUNITIVE SUBTYPES

Diligent—or Micromanager

People who display this pattern tend to be perfectionists, more focused on tactical execution than the big picture, taking conscientiousness to an extreme. They downplay their own accomplishments, and accept or give credit only when "perfection" has been achieved. Because they are so concerned about being criticized, they are reluctant to try new approaches and often suffer from "analysis paralysis." As a result, they may spend so much time obsessively scrutinizing plans that they never actually implement them. Just as they blame themselves harshly when they make mistakes, they also closely examine others' work for small errors and are quick to blame them. Not only do they assign credit and blame in a black-and-white, "all or nothing" manner, they also blame people not just for what they do or don't achieve, but also for how they perform their work. If a "diligent" type receives the slightest blame from their superiors, they are likely to criticize and blame subordinates even more than usual, passing the blame down the line. Like their manager, teams that work for this kind of boss can become so preoccupied with details that they neglect the bigger picture, and miss the forest for the trees.

Dutiful—or Martyr

Dutiful types are more focused on pleasing their superiors than on supporting their subordinates. They "bask in reflected glory" when their superiors are credited for an accomplishment, but are uncomfortable accepting any credit themselves. They require a lot of reassurance from their superiors that they are doing a good job, and become unduly upset if not credited or appreciated by a boss. They take more blame than they deserve in order to preserve working relationships, even accepting blame for others' mistakes, sometimes pleasantly surprising those who actually made the mistakes. They also blame themselves in a harsh, self-critical manner that serves to deflect others' criticism.

WHAT TO DO?

Working with or for people who fit into each of these types can be among the most difficult, unpleasant, and challenging workplace experiences one can have. So much about whether our jobs are satisfying or miserable is determined by our relationship with our immediate boss and co-workers. If these people tend toward one of these types—or are extreme cases or a blend of several of them—there's no question that it's a truly trying situation. So, what do you do if you are working closely with someone who falls into one of these categories?

First of all, it's important to keep in mind that you want to think first, and then tread carefully in addressing the problem. As an executive coach, clients often ask me, "How do I get the credit I deserve?" or, "How can I stop my boss or colleagues from stealing credit for my ideas?" I always caution that there is no fail-safe, "one size fits all" approach to these issues. Any suggestion, such as, "Take on a more visible leadership role," or, "Cultivate your network in the organization so that people other than your boss are aware of what you are achieving," entails risk. By becoming more visible, you might anger or threaten your boss, who might come to see you as a rival. By cultivating your internal network, you might get enmeshed in organizational politics. In my experience, executive coaches can be as helpful by encouraging their clients to do nothing as by encouraging them to take action. Simply asking a client, "Is that really what you want to do?" can often be extremely helpful, especially since, as we've seen, credit and blame can cause us to become overly emotional and to act in impulsive and intemperate ways.

Therefore, before making any moves to try to right what you perceive to be a wrong, first try to look at your situation from a more "objective" vantage point. Ask yourself if the state you're in may be influencing how you are viewing the situation. Paradoxically, in order to see your situation more objectively, the most helpful thing is to understand and "correct for" your own subjective filters of credit and blame. One way to do this is to look at the arc of issues that you have wrestled with and tried to master over the course of your career, and to consider what is similar and what is different about yourself, your boss, your colleagues, your team, and your organization in this current situation as compared to others you have experienced in the past.

Helpful questions you may ask yourself can include, "Am I seeing this situation in a biased way?" "What is being triggered for me in this situation?" "Am I being overly sensitive, anxious, or reactive?" or, "Even though I feel unfairly credited and blamed, might there be some way in which I can learn from this experience?"

Interpersonal chemistry is based on a complex interplay of human "traits" and "states." It may be that your boss is blaming you because she is a chronic blamer, and/or because she's having a bad day, and it may bother you too much because you are overly sensitive, and/or because *you're* having a bad day. At a certain point for all of us, the quantity of blame that we receive can impact the quality of the blame that we experience. Or being deprived of credit one day might not bother us, while on another day we might be very bothered about the same oversight or slight. An ordinary straw one day might be the last straw the next day. Taking a step back, formulating hypotheses, and testing them over time is almost always a better strategy than rushing to judgment or immediately leaping into action. While it can be difficult to make the dynamics of credit and blame better, it's actually very easy to make them worse.

Another important factor to consider is whether in stressful situations, when you and/or the people who work for you are under pressure, you yourself might display, or be perceived as displaying, some of the attributes of these dysfunctional types. As we considered earlier, there is a high degree of subjectivity when it comes to credit and blame. Even if we have the best of intentions in how we give and get credit and blame, others may see us as having problematic traits or even as fitting into one of the dysfunctional types. Therefore, it's important to try to stay attuned to others' perceptions of your approach by reflecting and soliciting feedback, so that you can identify and, when necessary, attempt to remedy others' emerging perceptions before they become established conclusions.

KNOW THYSELF

It's important to try to evaluate yourself in the same way, using the same criteria and standards, that you use to evaluate others. Knowing our strengths and weaknesses is itself an extremely important strength. However, self-knowledge of our personalities or types in general, or in the area of credit and blame in particular, is not easy for any of us to achieve.

It's always much easier to see how others' personalities impact their behavior and reactions than it is to understand our own personalities. When it comes to other people, we can often clearly see consistent patterns of overestimating their own contributions, or underestimating how much they have been helped by circumstance, luck, or other people. We can also see how our friends and co-workers undervalue the amount of credit they receive from others, and overreact to the blame they get. It may be clear to us that a friend or valued colleague is being more sensitive about not having been credited, or more defensive about having been blamed, than is warranted. Not only is it clear to us that our friend has misread or misinterpreted the situation; it's also clear to us that, even if her interpretations were true, she is acting contrary to her own interests. She may go too far in trying to rationalize a minor mistake, or fight too hard for credit that isn't worth very much. Or perhaps we clearly see how much our friend internalizes the credit or blame she receives from others, and therefore how fragile and vulnerable she may be if she is working for a toxic boss or on a dysfunctional team.

Seeing ourselves with such clarity is another thing altogether. But people who master the dynamics of credit and blame cultivate self-knowledge to the point where they can perceive their own tendencies with the same perspective and accuracy that they have in observing others' and remain focused on the long term. Self-knowledge and a thoughtful and balanced approach to giving and getting credit and blame go hand-in-hand.

Self-knowledge can sometimes be made use of in the wrong ways, however. It should be used for explanation, not for justification. For example, instead of thinking, "I can't blame myself for not having a better professional network; after all, I'm very introverted," it's more helpful to think, "Networking is hard for me, so I need to find strategies that work for me." And it's not useful to think, "I'm a dutiful type, so that's why I don't seek out or accept credit"; it's more helpful to think, "I may be too humble and self-effacing, and that may end up being a problem for me and my team."

In considering whether you or the people you work with or for may have some of these traits, keep in mind that everyone has much more control over how they personally react to credit and blame, and how they dispense both, than they have over how anyone else does. Therefore, in problematic situations, first consider how you can take a different approach yourself, before you start trying to get others to see things differently or convincing them to take a different approach.

Of course, the problem may simply be unsolvable, for various reasons. The stories I told about Robert, Genna, and Katerina have happy endings; but there are certainly some situations where it is just not possible to deal with a dysfunctional boss, colleague, or subordinate, or where your own style simply will not work. Over the years, I have coached several clients who ultimately were not able to successfully influence their bosses, and who ended up transferring inside their companies or even leaving their organizations. If a boss consistently exhibits a dysfunctional pattern and is unresponsive to your new approach, in some unfortunate cases the only thing you can do is "leave the field" and take your talents and skills elsewhere. A boss's dysfunctional pattern of credit and blame might actually be a symptom of (or even encouraged by) organizational politics that you not only cannot control, but may not even be able to observe or influence at all.

If you are convinced that you are being undervalued by your boss, at a certain point you may conclude that you will only receive fair recognition and compensation by leaving the organization. But before you do, you should seriously consider the broad set of dynamics that may be at play in the larger situation. Viewing the way you are treated as reflecting factors that go well beyond your boss's personality can provide a helpful perspective. Perhaps your boss is just rational and self-interested, rather than crazy and cruel. What may feel like a psychodrama might actually be quite a rational unfolding of events.

One way to look at the credit and blame that you receive from your organization is that it actually is an accurate reflection of *something*, even if not of your contributions. Also, while it's easy to get stuck in a rut and remain in a situation where you chronically blame your boss for being unfair, it's also possible to use feeling "screwed" and helpless in a positive way. Instead of blaming your boss, you could hold yourself responsible for tolerating the situation and not taking the risks or proactive steps that might change your situation. You can think to yourself, "This undervaluation is a great signal that I need to work harder, learn more, build my political base inside the organization, and build my network outside of the organization. When I begin to receive more credit and less blame from my boss, that will not only reflect my actual efforts and contributions but also be reflective of my success in these other realms."

People are often surprised to see how much patterns of credit and blame can change over time. Sometimes, quitting may be a permanent solution to a temporary problem. And even in the unfortunate situations where the only solution is to leave, it's still helpful to take a learning approach and try to gain self-awareness, which can help you avoid, or better manage, similar situations in the future. In that event, understanding how you personally react to others' patterns of credit and blame can be a huge help in making future moves. I'll address this more fully in chapter 7, and will suggest strategies that you can use to cope with a boss or colleague who is particularly challenging.

As you think about the personality types that have been introduced in this chapter, it's important to keep in mind that even if a boss or colleague perfectly fits one or another of them (or some combination thereof), this doesn't mean that you have just solved the mystery of what's going on. First of all, your evaluation or categorization of your boss might not be widely shared, since other people may experience him or her differently in different situations, or even differently in the same situations. Second, even if your categorization of your boss is fully shared by everyone else around you, the meaning of the boss's behavior, and the impact on others, will vary for every individual on your team. And finally, even if you and everyone around you are in full agreement, at all times, about a boss or a colleague's personality or type, why they are acting that way may still be a mystery.

The most helpful strategy is to take a learning approach. Learn about your boss, learn about the situation, and learn about yourself. Hopefully, the personality dimensions and types I have presented will provide you with a helpful framework for considering the "whats" of your boss's or colleague's behavior, even if you have to get to know something of their stories, and to empathize with them, in order to truly begin to understand the "whys." If you walk a mile in their moccasins, you may not just see them differently, you may also reconsider why they see you, and credit and blame you, the way they do. Learning to understand others' "whys" and our own is both crucial and a career-long challenge.

Because of the complex personal, interpersonal, and social psychology of credit and blame, it's always hard to untangle the relationship between people and situations. In this chapter, we've started with the "person" side of the equation, describing personality dimensions and types, and considered how situational factors influence people and their interactions. In the next chapter we will examine the other side, considering how situations can be particularly influential in causing people to behave badly when it comes to credit and blame.

CHAPTER 4

Situational Awareness

Because we are so inclined to attribute people's behavior to personality, we tend to underestimate the importance of situations in influencing, or even determining, that behavior. People who are normally quite different from one another may act similarly in certain situations, for instance, when they are accused of making a mistake. By the same token, the same person may behave quite differently in different situations, for example, at home versus the office. A person who at home or with friends has no inclination at all to become accusatory may transform into a vicious "blame-thrower" at the office under pressure. We might be supportive, lenient, and forgiving to co-workers with whom we have good chemistry and history, and relentlessly harsh on people who rub us the wrong way for whatever reason, or with whom our working relationships started off on the wrong foot. Or, we might be supportive and nonaccusatory to those within our own work team, or on allied work teams, but quick to blame people who work on other teams, particularly teams that our own has issues with.

If we're confronting a credit deficit or a blame surplus at work, it is vital that we consider how a range of situational influences might be at play. Not only will this be invaluable for navigating our way through the danger zones for ourselves, but it will make us much better colleagues to, and leaders of, others. We should always keep in mind that in determining human behavior the situation may matter as much as, or even more than, the attributes of the people. This realization empowers us to choose or help build a workplace that discourages blame and encourages cooperation.

Some of the situational influences on our behavior are fairly straightforward and obvious, though we may not manage to keep them in mind enough on a daily basis. Others are quite hidden: subconscious triggers that can be very difficult to become aware of. The good news about the situational influences we'll look into is that there are ways to intervene that can transform negative dynamics into positive ones. It's incredibly hard to change "traits" in ourselves or others, but there is much more opportunity to positively influence our "states" and those of others, first by becoming aware of the importance of the social situations we work in, and then by working to constructively influence those situations.

Unfortunately, in too many offices and workplaces, people find themselves working in situations that encourage blame, with incentives for blaming, that resemble a "Prisoner's Dilemma."

BLAME AND/OR BE BLAMED

In 1950, Albert W. Tucker, an acclaimed mathematician, coined the phrase "Prisoner's Dilemma" to describe a situation that vividly illustrates just how dramatically our behavior can be shaped by the situation we find ourselves in. In its classic form, the scenario unfolds as follows:

Let's say that the police arrest you and a friend, but they have insufficient evidence with which to convict the two of you. The first thing the officers do is separate you and your friend by placing you into different rooms where you can't see or communicate with each other. Then, the officers visit each room and make you and your friend the same offer: "If you agree to testify against your buddy, you'll go free." If both of you remain silent, each refusing to "rat" each other out, you will each spend only one year in jail. If you both agree to testify, thus solidifying your joint guilt, you will each spend three years in a prison cell. If your buddy decides to testify against you while you remain silent, however, you will receive a full 10-year sentence to prison while he walks out the door. Your choice is simple: speak up or stay silent. But so much is riding on what your friend decides to do. What do you do?[1]

We find ourselves in analogous situations in the workplace all the time—especially when things go wrong and tensions run high. Perhaps a mistake has been made and your boss wants to know whether it was your fault, your co-worker's fault, or if both of you are to blame. To find out, she invites each of you into her office, separately, for a chat. You have an incentive in this situation to blame your co-worker, because by doing so, you might either receive a reduced punishment or get off the hook entirely.

In the classic Prisoner's Dilemma scenario, turning in your friend is called "defecting." The tricky part of this response is that if you and your friend both act selfishly by defecting, you both end up worse off than if you had stayed silent. When you both defect, the police end up with evidence against both of you. By contrast, the optimal joint outcome for the two of you is achieved only if you both cooperate with one another by staying silent, which will ensure that you each receive light sentences. To pull this off, though, you must trust one another, and this is hard to do in such a situation, with the threat of jail looming— or, in the case of work, the fear of being chastised, demoted, or fired. In other words, the best shared outcome for the two of you can only be achieved in the presence of trust. In a workplace where the tendency is to blame, individuals rarely trust each other enough to achieve the "maximum joint utility."

The standard Prisoner's Dilemma is, of course, an extreme scenario. In the real world, few bosses would resort to such a procedure for determining blame. But the basic point that trust is necessary for collaboration and the best outcome is still a helpful one, and it's also true that a highly punitive approach to managing, in which a boss is always on the lookout for who is to blame, will tend to produce a culture of defecting rather than one of cooperating between employees. It may seem in such a situation that there is no way out, that casting the blame on someone else is the only way to go, but it's helpful to always keep in mind that you do in fact have another choice: you can opt to risk accepting blame yourself. This can, in fact, be a very powerful choice, especially over the longer term, because although a lack of trust can cause people to cast blame, taking blame can actually build trust.

This is illustrated powerfully by a variation on the Prisoner's Dilemma scenario, one that is a closer approximation to the actual situation we're most often in at the office. This variation is called the "Iterated Prisoner's Dilemma," and was described by Robert Axelrod in his book *The Evolution of Cooperation*. Whereas the classic Prisoner's Dilemma is a one-shot deal, in this version the players continue to play round after round, which gives them the chance to reward or punish their opponents for their prior decisions.[2] People playing this form of the game tend to adapt a "tit-for-tat" strategy, which entails either defecting or cooperating based on your opponent's last move. If your co-worker blamed you in the prior round of your boss calling you into her office, for example, you would blame him this time around, or, if your co-worker blamed himself last time, you would in turn cooperate by blaming yourself. The more you reciprocate in this way, the more trust is built between you.

Like the bats mentioned in chapter 1, we remember how our co-workers have acted toward us in the past, which affects our level of trust and willingness to cooperate with them in the present and the future. Axelrod found that when people played the game for long periods of time, those using "greedy" strategies—always defecting regardless of what the other player did—suffered in the long run. So did those who were always cooperative, since greedy opponents consistently took advantage of them. Those players who played using more adaptive strategies, on the other hand, such as rewarding a cooperative opponent by cooperating in subsequent rounds, prospered by comparison.

If you find yourself in a situation like this at work, where you and your co-workers are regularly being expected to explain who was at fault for something, strategically deciding to accept some of the blame some of the time can be a highly effective way to gain the trust of colleagues, to focus on problem solving, and to prevent a vicious cycle of blame from kicking in. What was particularly noteworthy in Axelrod's study is that when players use cooperation more often in early stages of the game, it can become contagious—thus building more trusting expectations over time. Individuals who "self-sacrifice" in earlier rounds by cooperating, even though they recognize the odds are that their opponent will defect, can actually help to significantly tip the balance.

If a co-worker of yours sees that you aren't seeking to throw him under a bus and act only in your own short-term self-interest, he will likely begin to reciprocate with cooperative moves of his own. The more members of an organization behave in this way, the better the chances that the workplace will become more trusting and cooperative over the long term, so that people focus on getting work done instead of on blaming each other for why it isn't getting done. Of course, another lesson here is that if you are the leader of a team or organization, you can also do a great deal to ensure that your employees don't perceive that they are in a blame-encouraging Prisoner's Dilemma in the first place.

GROUPTHINK

Another of the powerful situational influences that can lead to blame getting out of control in the office is a type of bonding and social dynamic that too often happens within groups. The members of a department or a team, for example, may become collectively defensive and see issues from a biased perspective, which can result in pointing the finger at others rather than constructively critiquing their own performance. This is a phenomenon known as *groupthink*. The term was coined by William H. Whyte, author of *The Organization Man*,[3] in a 1952 issue of *Fortune*, and it was popularized by the psychologist Irving Janis, who studied its role in historical events such as the failure to anticipate the attack on Pearl Harbor or the decision to break into Watergate, where small, isolated groups of like-minded people made bad decisions to disastrous effect.

As James Surowiecki explains in his book *The Wisdom of Crowds*:

> Homogeneous groups become more cohesive more easily than diverse groups, and as they become more cohesive they become more dependent on the group, more isolated from outside opinions, and therefore more convinced that the group's judgment on important issues must be right. These kinds of groups, Janis suggested, share an illusion of invulnerability, a willingness to rationalize away counterarguments to the group's position, and a conviction that dissent is not useful.[4]

Surowiecki suggests that in order for a group to make good decisions and avoid groupthink, its members must first reach their own independent opinions. He argues that the best decisions are made by groups populated by individuals with a diversity of opinions, so that more angles and possibilities are considered. True wisdom results from aggregating and combining a multitude of individual perspectives to arrive at the best collective decision.

When groups fail to embrace diversity and decentralization, there is always the potential to end up with groupthink, which is the opposite of "the Wisdom of Crowds." Consider the Columbia space shuttle disaster, in which NASA's rigid hierarchy did not solicit sufficient input from lower-ranking scientists, even though they likely had the most firsthand knowledge of the problems at hand. The group's decision-making process involved premature consensus and a failure to consider alternative approaches that might have saved the crew.

In groupthink, people influence each other to go along with the real or perceived consensus, to censor themselves, and neglect to raise or consider objections to planned courses of action. The effects of groupthink on individuals can be astonishing. Consider the work done by the psychologist Solomon Asch at Swarthmore College. He asked groups of people to compare the length of several lines printed on index cards and then judge which was the longest. The results revealed that many subjects reported actually seeing shorter lines as being longer based on the perceptions first expressed by the majority of the group, who were in fact experimental "confederates."[5]

Management expert Jerry Harvey used a story to illustrate the dynamics of groupthink, identifying what he dubbed the Abilene Paradox.[6] In his story, a group of four people talks about what they want to do on a hot and dusty summer day. When one member suggests that they could drive to Abilene, a town several hours away, the rest of the group members agree to go there. At the end of the day, after they return from their trip, which none of them enjoyed, each person realizes they never wanted to go to Abilene in the first place—not even the individual who suggested it.

When it comes to issues of credit and blame, groupthink can lead teams of people to take credit that's not due and to become highly defensive and persecutory toward others in the organization over failures. The group members rally around one another and become biased, unable to perceive things that they might be doing wrong. In essence, the group has developed a kind of egotistical "personality" of its own; it suffers from self-serving bias, distorts facts, and denies reality. It is then quite easy for groups to come into conflict with one another, each pushing the other further into groupthink. When this occurs, it becomes difficult for leaders to break the escalating cycle of blame and contagious threat-rigidity effects.

Envision the following scenario: You're hired to run a well-known company and you're suddenly presented with a great opportunity to open a whole new market by introducing a breakthrough new product. To pull it off, you ask your sales and product development teams to collaborate on the effort. Unfortunately, the endeavor is not a success and your company suffers a huge loss in productivity. As a result, your two teams begin pointing fingers at each other to assign blame. Never particularly friendly to begin with, the members of each team begin to avoid each other in the halls and around the coffeepot. Companywide meetings take on a nasty tone of "us" versus "them," with attendees sitting in departmental cliques. Frustrated, you decide to get to the bottom of things by separately taking the head of each of the departments out to lunch. After listening to each person plead their case about why their department wasn't to blame, and the other department was, you begin to hear similar phrases like, "All they want to do is close the sale, they don't care about quality," or, "They never listened to us—they only wanted to build what they decided to build and not what the client wanted to buy." According to each of your department leaders, then, the fault for failure lies clearly in the shortcomings of the other group.

A scenario very much like this one awaited Carlos Ghosn when he took the job of turning around Nissan, the Japanese auto company. When Ghosn made the decision to move to Tokyo in March 1999, the company was struggling. But it wasn't just that its cars weren't selling; it seemed that interdepartmental strife was threatening to tear Nissan apart. A "deep-seated cultural problem we had to address was the organization's inability to accept responsibility," Ghosn wrote in a 2001 *Harvard Business Review* article. "We had a culture of blame. If the company did poorly, it was always someone else's fault. Sales blamed product planning, product planning blamed engineering, and engineering blamed finance. Tokyo blamed Europe, and Europe blamed Tokyo."[7]

The intergroup conflicts Ghosn described at Nissan happen every day in companies all over the world. Members of groups inadvertently fall into a trap psychologists call the *ultimate attribution error*.[8] Simply put, this is a dynamic where we attribute the same qualities or personality characteristics to most, if not all, of the members of a group, and then proceed to make attributions about behavior based on these presumed dispositions rather than the situation at hand.

In the contemporary American workplace, it is unlikely that anyone would blatantly claim that it was members of a certain racial, ethnic, generational, religious, or gender group who were to blame for the organization's ills. If an individual did make such claims openly, a senior manager or HR would soon arrive at the scene to provide a reminder of company policies, government regulations, and cultural norms against such discrimination. However, if an individual in one department rails against members of some other department, even if he or she is openly making claims and drawing conclusions based on departmental scapegoating or stereotyping, it is much less likely that a manager or an HR professional will intervene. In my experience, interdepartmental rivalries can easily begin to resemble racism or xenophobia, and even the legendary family feud that pitted the Hatfields against the McCoys.

Instead of Hatfields, it may be the sales team, and instead of McCoys, it may be the product development team. Members of the sales team can fall into the habit of thinking that all product developers are the same, focused only on what they want to build instead of what customers actually want to buy. At the same time, the product developers may assume that all members of the sales team are singularly focused on trying to sell more and more merchandise, regardless of profit margins, costs, or consequences.

When we are not personally embroiled in the heat of an interteam conflict, it's easy to see how unproductive and potentially damaging this kind of thinking can be. But what makes group-based blinders so dangerous is that we often don't even realize when we're wearing them ourselves. The "group-serving bias" is a self-serving bias that operates on a collective, rather than an individual, basis. As the psychologist David DeSteno told the *New York Times*, "Anyone who is on 'our team' is excused for moral transgressions. The importance of group cohesion, of any type, simply extends our moral radius for lenience . . . One person's patriot is another's terrorist."[9]

We overlook errors and omissions made by members of our own group, but see others' with crystal clarity. In an experiment conducted by the psychologists Albert Hartorf and Hadley Cantril in 1954, Princeton and Dartmouth students were shown a filmstrip of a controversial football game played between the two schools. Students were asked to count the number of infractions or actions worthy of a penalty committed by each side.

Not surprisingly, the Princeton students counted many more infractions among the Dartmouth players; the Dartmouth students, on the other hand, thought the Princeton players were the ones playing dirty. The researchers concluded that "There is no such 'thing' as a 'game' existing 'out there' in its own right which people merely 'observe.' . . . For the 'thing' simply is not the same for different people whether the 'thing' is a football game, a presidential candidate, Communism, or spinach."[10]

Another study that illuminated important dynamics involved in groupthink and intergroup rivalry was conducted by Muzafer Sherif of the University of Oklahoma; it has come to be known as the Robber's Cave Experiment.[11] Sherif and his team selected twenty-four normal and well-adjusted twelve-year-olds from the area around Robber's Cave State Park in Oklahoma. The idea of the experiment was to separate the boys into two randomly assigned teams, gradually introduce the teams to each other through a series of competitions that involved prizes, and then observe what happened. The result sounds like a plot line out of *Lord of the Flies*, *West Side Story*, or even the basis for a reality show about summer camp gone bad. Before long, the two teams had given themselves names, the Rattlers and the Eagles, and not only began taunting each other during the competitions, but also began raiding and pillaging each other's camps and trying to capture and then burn the rival flag. Very often in business, too, groups yield to the unproductive temptation to see the world in black-and-white terms, crediting themselves and blaming others.

RUMBLE IN MANHATTAN

Consider the case of the corporate merger between AOL and Time Warner, which not only remains the largest of its kind in

American business history but has also gone down as one of the greatest business disasters of all time. Finalized on January 10, 2000, the deal, which was valued at $350 billion at the time, shocked the world.[12] Not just the size of the deal impressed, but so did the companies themselves: AOL, the upstart Internet service provider that was enabling some 27 million adults, children, and grandmothers alike (40 percent of everyone online at the time) to surf the web and check their email; and Time Warner, the esteemed giant of the media world's old guard, were joining forces. The optimists saw it as a merger of equals, where Time Warner's vast entertainment library—consisting of record labels, TV and movie studios, television networks, and book and magazine publishing divisions—would be paired with the New Economy's preferred delivery service: the Internet. It was a dream match, at least in theory. Yet, ten years after the merger was announced, the companies split over irreconcilable differences—both seemingly worse off for the experience. As of January 10, 2010, the combined worth of the two companies was just one seventh of what it was the day the deal was announced, meaning that the combined company, ten years later, was 86 percent less valuable than the sum of its parts had been on merger day. In fact, by 2003 the holdings of the company's biggest shareholder, Ted Turner, had gone down an astounding $8 billion (80 percent) and he had also left his job as vice chairman "in disgust."[13]

There is no shortage of business case studies that have asked and endeavored to explain what went wrong. Possible culprits or scapegoats include the two executives who shepherded the deal, Steve Case from AOL and Gerald Levin from Time Warner, as well as other feuding senior executives from the two legacy companies. Possible reasons include the failure to maximize the value of Time Warner's content through AOL's online channels, the bursting of the dot-com bubble, and even the evolution of the Internet itself, as AOL's dial-up access quickly became outdated when high-speed options became more affordable and available much more rapidly than had been anticipated. Another explanation provided by many involved in the combined company is that the two corporate cultures were a mismatch from the beginning. It seemed that AOL employees were soon pitted against Time Warner staffers in an internal turf war. As an article in the *New York Times* put it: "Both sides seemed to hate each other." Quotes from executives on either side, reflecting in hindsight on the logic behind the deal, seem to support this description. Richard D. Parsons, Time Warner's president at the time of the merger, said: "I remember saying at a vital board meeting where we approved this, that life was going to be different going forward because they're very different cultures, but I have to tell you, I underestimated how different." And Ted Leonsis, then a divisional vice president at AOL, based at the time in Dulles, Virginia, said: "The news release that they showed us and the positioning was that AOL would be the crown jewel, and I'd say, 'Well, if we're the crown jewel, why are all our best and most important people leaving here and going to New York?'"[14]

Part of the problem was the cultural ingredients in the merger; but the way the story unfolded created the recipe for disaster. As the merger failed to live up to its potential, executives from the two legacy companies began to blame one another, creating a vicious cycle of unproductive finger-pointing and mutual recrimination. The focus on blame created an environment in which the kind of collaboration and creativity that might have helped the combined company live up to its potential was not realized. Employees from both sides fell victim to the negative between-group dynamics, which created an "us" versus "them" environment at just the time when cooperation and collaboration were paramount.

However, not every two groups that come into contact will necessarily suffer such a negative fate. Even groups that are drifting apart can be brought together again. We can see one effective strategy for doing so by revisiting Sherif's Robber's Cave Experiment. Just as he was curious to see how the boys participating in his study would begin to compete or come into conflict, Sherif also wanted to see if he could find ways to unify the two groups after they had begun to antagonize each other. After observing the tribal warfare between the Rattlers and the Eagles for several days, Sherif's researchers experimented with how they might change the way the participants thought of their rival group. While simple efforts to get the two groups of boys to socialize with each other by watching a movie or shooting off fireworks failed, adding an outside "enemy" that forced the groups to work together proved successful.

In this case, the researchers stopped the flow of fresh water to both camps, blaming vandals. The two teams suddenly had a common mission—to get the water flowing again—and they quickly united. Once they got the water flowing, the two teams even showed civility toward each other for the first time. And, in the end, after all the early disputes that pitted the two groups of boys against one another, the achievement of solving the water crisis along with a few other similar exercises brought the boys closer together. As they headed home after the experiment was concluded, they even elected to all ride in the same bus—in many cases, Rattlers and Eagles sitting happily side by side. The use of common objectives can be an effective means of converting a mind-set that pits "us" against "them" into one of "we."

Setting "superordinate goals"—goals that will benefit the entire collectivity of people, not just one group or the other—can not only help groups of young campers collaborate, it can also be an effective tool for overcoming negative intergroup dynamics in the workplace. As an example, let's look back at what happened at Nissan after Ghosn took over. He was successful in turning around Nissan and the company began making better cars and operating more efficiently—transforming what was a business losing millions into one that was earning billions. This achievement is a credit to Ghosn's courage and willingness to blast apart the traditional corporate hierarchy Nissan had grown accustomed to, which he replaced with a matrix of cross-functional and even cross-company teams that injected a new sense of diversity and collegiality throughout the organization—something particularly bold at a Japanese company at that time. By creating eleven teams constituted of people from different departments, particularly those that had been prone to fall into blaming patterns with each other in the past, and then giving them shared performance goals, such as reducing their material costs by 20 percent, Ghosn set "superordinate goals" throughout the entire Nissan organization and held members of different groups individually and collectively accountable for achieving them. Where once a department head would be quick to blame a counterpart in another division of the company, he or she now was part of the same group charged with achieving the same goal, and was therefore much more likely to focus on fixing things than on wasting time, energy, and goodwill in blaming.

Of course, overcoming intergroup conflicts and the powerful influence of the ultimate attribution error isn't as simple as rearranging an organization chart. It often requires a great deal of effort and perhaps even some trial and error and experimentation. To help demonstrate how to identify and overcome this problem, consider the following case study of a cosmetics company at which I helped reduce intergroup conflict and counteract the ultimate attribution error in their workplace.

My former client, which I will call "Spritz Co.," had built a successful business by building a prestigious brand. As the company grew, it was easy to attract and retain talented executives, particularly in the marketing department, which was viewed as the engine of growth. However, as the company matured, growth slowed, and it became more difficult to recruit and retain talented marketing executives. As a result, the marketing department and the HR department were at odds with one another.

Communication and cooperation had broken down completely. There were many open positions in the marketing department and senior management had begun to ask what was going on. "We need to fill these positions to help with our upcoming initiatives," the CEO remarked, also asking, "How can it be so hard to find enough good people?" The marketing department blamed the HR department, claiming that HR had failed to provide a sufficient number of qualified candidates. To make matters worse, the few qualified candidates who had come in lost interest when they didn't hear back from the company for several weeks after their interviews. HR, on the other hand, blamed the marketing team, claiming that they hadn't provided job descriptions or even taken the time to provide sufficient feedback about candidates who had been interviewed. Interestingly, in the few cases where positions had been filled, both departments jockeyed to take credit. The managers from marketing described how they had used their personal networks to find candidates, bypassing HR's recruiting function. Meanwhile, HR described how they had found candidates using online search tools because they were given no good leads by marketing.

At Spritz Co., HR got along better with the finance department than with the marketing department. The people working in the HR and finance departments generally treated one another with consideration and respect. These good feelings, something psychologists call *positivity*, were due in part to the good working relationships between the leaders of the two departments, as well as a function of an earlier history of collaboration.

The positive history between HR and finance, and the negative history between HR and marketing, also caused different interpretations of, and explanations for, the same behaviors depending on which department someone was from. For example, if a finance person didn't provide feedback about a candidate after an interview, the HR people would attribute this to the finance person's busy schedule, and simply make a note and ask them for it the next time they encountered the interviewer. However, if a marketing person didn't provide post-interview feedback, the HR people would perceive that they had been "dissed," and would send threatening emails demanding feedback, citing rules that if feedback was not forthcoming, there would be a delay in scheduling the next batch of candidates. The marketing people didn't appreciate these threatening communications, and became even more reluctant to give HR candidate evaluations. Therefore, for HR, receiving feedback from marketing became the exception rather than the rule. Because the managers in finance generally provided their evaluations after interviews, HR credited them with being good organizational citizens, and perceived that receiving feedback from finance was the rule rather than the exception. And, since the marketing people only provided evaluations after being harangued, HR didn't credit them at all for doing so.

In the course of my consultation with Spritz Co., I helped them create a standard "process map" for the recruitment process, which enabled HR to keep track of metrics like "time to fill" for various positions. At first, there was some resistance to this idea on the HR team, as there was a concern that these metrics would only be used as another blame stick with which marketing could beat HR and criticize its performance. As in so many companies, people complain about blame and ambiguity, but then resist metrics and clarity. However, the courageous head of HR realized that these tracking mechanisms would also create accountability for marketing, because the system would include a record of if and when feedback had been received about the candidates provided by HR to marketing. The two departments agreed to feed information into a transparent system, which helped increase the flow of qualified candidates, and was a first step toward the two departments collaborating more broadly on recruiting and other activities.

As this case study shows, although establishing "superordinate goals" can be very powerful in reducing intergroup conflict, it may not always work. At Spritz Co. the HR team and the marketing department had a shared goal—to attract, recruit, and retain the most qualified candidates for the organization. But what was missing was accountability for progressing together toward that goal. Joint responsibility along the lines of what Carlos Ghosn created at Nissan with the cross-functional teams can be the extra catalyst for cooperation. In essence, this means that a leader who is senior to the heads of the feuding departments can essentially say something like: "Rather than spending countless hours trying to go back in time to assign blame to the marketing and HR teams to determine why we've had such a hard time filling these positions, I'm going to hold you individually and collectively accountable for significantly speeding up 'time to fill' for open positions, and for taking proactive steps to assist each other in achieving this goal." Because Ghosn, as the leader, changed the situation in which the teams were working, he helped stop, and then reverse, the negative feedback loops that threatened the whole enterprise.

SELF-FULFILLING PROPHECIES

A further set of strong situational influences on the dynamics of credit and blame and workplace behavior and performance are the expectations that others have of us, and often impose on us. What can often happen is that either a boss or a colleague projects onto us what she believes to be the truth. The fateful effect is that this projection can lead us to behave accordingly. In this case, our boss or co-worker has created a self-fulfilling prophecy.

The classic story of a self-fulfilling prophecy is that of Pygmalion. In Ovid's tale, Pygmalion sets out to carve a statue of the ideal woman out of a block of ivory. He is then so taken with his creation that he falls in love with her, going so far as to beg the goddess Venus to bring the sculpture to life, which Venus agrees to do, and the two live happily ever after.

Psychologists now use the term *Pygmalion effect* to refer to the phenomenon by which people live up, or down, to the expectations of others. The researchers Robert Rosenthal and Lenore Jacobson published a seminal article on this effect in 1968, in which they described a study involving elementary school students.[15] Teachers were told that some students were especially talented and bright, though these so-called special students had been chosen at random. The result was that the "bright" students ended up performing better in school, and getting higher scores on tests, because of their teachers' positive expectations. The researchers found that if teachers thought students were gifted, they gave those students more attention and assistance, which then helped fulfill the prophecy that the students were indeed talented. The opposite was also true. If a student was labeled an underachiever, poor test results confirmed the label, despite the fact that they were randomly assigned to the group and their previous tests had showed they were capable students.

In keeping with this process, others' expectations about the credit or blame that we are due can exert powerful influence in determining our actual performance. This happens in a three-step fashion, according to researchers Saul Kassin, Steve

Fein, and Hazel Rose Markus.[16] The first step is where a perceiver forms an impression of someone, maybe something like: "That guy is lazy and unmotivated." The perceiver then behaves toward that person in a way congruent with the perception: "I won't ask him to take on this extra project because he won't want to do it." And finally, the person unwittingly changes his or her behavior to meet the perceiver's expectations: "Everyone has already determined that I'm unmotivated and uninterested in doing extra work, and taking on new projects isn't going to change that perception." This process can work both ways, leading to positive or negative dynamics and results.

When your boss decides that you are a poor performer and prone to making mistakes, you will likely become more defensive and self-conscious, and you may even begin to make more mistakes—which will then confirm his initial impression of you. If, on the other hand, you are a favored member of your boss's staff, you might find yourself not only performing better but may even become the recipient of some unexpected credit, which helps fulfill the image of you as the office superstar, whether you really merit the designation or not. Unfortunately, upward spirals of credit are much less common than downward spirals of blame.

INSEAD professors Jean-François Manzoni and Jean-Louis Barsoux have identified this same negative dynamic between bosses and their subordinates, and termed it the "Set Up to Fail Syndrome," which became the title of their book on this subject. As Manzoni and Barsoux describe it:

> Most bosses faced with a seemingly poor performer begin to pay extra attention to the employee's work. Deprived of elbowroom the employee starts to feel frustrated and under-appreciated, often responding by reducing unnecessary contact with the boss. Thinking, mistakenly, that the subordinate's withdrawal confirms that she is indeed a weaker performer, the boss begins to

increase her involvement in the employee's affairs. Progressively, the subordinate begins to doubt her own thinking and ability. This ugly cycle continues until a perfectly capable employee gives up any dream of making a meaningful contribution to the company. The employee has been successfully set up to fail.[17]

I once helped a client combat this dynamic when I worked with the talented chief technology officer of an Internet start-up. He had hired me because he wanted to gain a better understanding of how he interacted with his team. Based on "360-degree" feedback that I collected by interviewing his colleagues and staff and presented to him, he realized that he had a tendency to make global categorizations of people as either competent or incompetent long before he had enough information to make an accurate judgment. Once categorized as incompetent, his subordinates felt uncredited and that their contributions were not valued, and they thought that they did not have the opportunity to change his negative opinions of them. They lost confidence and motivation and their performance suffered as a result.

During our meetings, we discussed his people and I would challenge him to see a more nuanced picture, inquiring about the shortcomings of some of his "stars" and the talents of some of the "dead wood." As a result of this coaching, the CTO learned not only that he was rushing to judgment but also that his judgments tended to become self-fulfilling. Over time, he learned to avoid making such premature judgments and started to give more specific, constructive feedback to his team. Instead of creating vicious cycles in which his staff's performance would get progressively worse, he began to focus more on credit than blame. By conveying confidence in his people, he was able to help them move up the learning curve instead of going down the drain.

RECIPROCAL
SELF-FULFILLING PROPHECIES

The dynamic by which a self-fulfilling prophecy can be visited upon us is fraught enough; but there is an even more complex way that people's expectations of one another can influence their behavior and become a form of self-fulfilling prophecy. A psychoanalytic concept identified by Melanie Klein that she called *projective identification* is illuminating.[18] In projective identification, two people first unconsciously "project" attributes onto one another, and then come to act toward each other in accordance with those projections. Generally, the attributes that people project onto the other person are attributes of the perceiver him- or herself that have been "split off" from the self and perceived in the other. The second step is that they each "identify" with or relate to one another's projections.[19] For example, if a subordinate subconsciously "projects" onto a boss that the boss is kind and supportive, the boss will sense these projections and "identify" with them, meaning that they confirm a view she has about herself, and likes to have of herself. It's as if the subordinate made a movie and cast the boss as a character, and then the boss watches the movie and thinks that the boss character accurately depicts her. Therefore, the subordinate is helping confirm the boss's hopes about herself and validating who she is.

Because the boss identifies with the positive projection, and wants to be more like the positive character in the subordinate's unconscious movie, the boss will become even more kind and supportive over time in response to the credit she is receiving. The boss may also come to see the subordinate as loyal and motivated, and the subordinate in turn identifies with those positive projections and acts to fulfill them.

Unfortunately, the dynamics of projective identification are not always positive. Depending on how the story between the boss and the subordinate unfolds, the subordinate may come to see the boss as cruel and abandoning, and the boss will likely pick up on these negative projections. Feeling blamed, the boss may identify with the negative projections, become angry, hurt, and hostile, and unconsciously start to act more like the wicked witch of the subordinate's psychodrama. At the same time, the boss may begin to see the subordinate as ungrateful and lazy, which may resonate with the subordinate's fears, and cause the subordinate to become less grateful and more lazy. Fortunately, it is possible to intervene in this process before it gets out of control.

THE BALANCING ACT
BETWEEN TWO AERIALISTS

A good example of how the dangers of projective identification can be avoided is the story of two performers I worked with, Laura and Angela, who are aerialists. My work with them was featured in the first episode of the PBS three-part series *This Emotional Life*.[20] The show they perform is awe-inspiring, and their story is a cautionary one, though ultimately hopeful too.

The incident that sent them to me for relationship counseling was dramatic. The audience went silent as the lights dimmed and two silvery threads, highlighted by a single beam of light, dropped from the ceiling. As the ribbons reached the floor, two lithe figures emerged from the shadows, prancing toward the center of the arena. Before anyone had a chance to blink, the two performers had hoisted themselves up into the air with superhuman speed. Gripping their respective tethers, they began a complicated series of spins and flips twenty-five feet in the air. To the astonishment of the crowd, Laura and Angela, who have been working together for more than ten years, began to spin in such a way that their twin ribbons intersected. Within seconds, the women leapt through the air into each other's arms, briefly embracing before reattaching themselves to their ribbons. Angela had recently designed this spectacular maneuver, which, if the partners had nailed it, would have taken their act to a whole new level. But as the two spun away from each other, Laura lost her grip, and the crowd's cheers turn to horrified gasps as she fell to the floor.

While Laura lay in a hospital bed recovering from a broken leg and elbow, she silently fumed at Angela. "Why did we have to change our routine?" she asked herself again and again. "We were successful with what we already did." In Laura's mind, Angela was clearly at fault for her injury. Why didn't Angela appreciate all the success they had achieved already? Why did she have to keep pushing to do something new? The more she brooded, the more Laura began to think that perhaps she would be better off finding a different partner, someone more interested in their financial future than in inventing new routines.

Meanwhile, Angela, who cried constantly while Laura was in the hospital, was wracked with guilt. At the same time, though, she was secretly angry. Angela was bored with their existing maneuvers and thought it time they challenged themselves with something new. She was particularly excited about the new routine and she had insisted to Laura that they insert it into their act. After hours of successfully practicing the new routine, she never thought they would fail. That sequence, if they had nailed it, could have elevated them into an act that rivaled international shows like Cirque du Soleil; instead, it brought them to the brink of ending their partnership.

"Laura never appreciated all the creativity I brought to our show each and every night," Angela complained. And the more she brooded, the more she wondered if she could even look at Laura again, let alone perform with her. "Why couldn't she pull off that flip when it counted?" she asked. Laura, in turn, resented being blamed, and came to defend herself and blame Angela. The two partners found themselves pitted against each other, trading blame in a hurtful and harmful way.

The dynamic that had taken hold was that Angela had projected onto Laura that she was a "bulldozer" who pushed a business agenda of sticking with their successful routine rather than trying new things, ignoring Angela's perspective. Laura, unconsciously sensing that she was being viewed this way, became even more strident and forceful. She came to see Angela as out of touch with economic necessity and less effective in handling planning and logistics. For her part, Angela began to blame herself for her lack of business acumen, and became even less secure and competent in handling those matters. Each was taking on the negative projections of the other, and this led to increasing tension and decreasing communication and collaboration.

Such a cycle of projective identification can be very difficult to break, but Laura and Angela's story has a happy ending. I helped them reach a "flipping point" in their relationship, where they began to understand that they each brought different and valuable skills to their partnership. I suggested they try switching roles for a while, with Angela handling the business side of things and Laura the creative tasks. For a high-profile performance for the national airline in El Salvador, they experimented with this approach, which they executed flawlessly. They found this a very helpful exercise, one that built their empathy for, and appreciation of, one another's talents and contributions. They soon realized that they hadn't given each other enough credit for the different gifts each contributed. Laura had the savvy organizational and promotional skills that allowed them to pull in a large crowd, while Angela had the enthusiasm and creativity to push for new aerial achievements to wow those crowds. The more discussions I facilitated for them, the more they realized that despite their shared disappointment about Laura's fall, they needed each other.

Although it's often tempting to try to intervene directly to fix a troubled workplace relationship, at times it can be very beneficial to take a less direct approach, and to first make a change, even a minor one, in the situation. By switching roles for even just one big show, Angela and Laura changed their working dynamic in a positive way that enabled them to begin rebuilding their relationship. Because the specifics of the situation at work can have so much to do with the finger-pointing that can erupt, even small changes in a situation can have a striking effect on reducing blame.

Situations in the workplace are fluid, and there are critical moments when the unfolding plot hangs in the balance. How each individual decides to act or react can alter the course of his or her relationships with others, as well as the dynamics within teams, or between teams. The further along the highway to blame a situation has traveled, and the more self-fulfilling dynamics have spiraled out of control, the more challenging it is for individuals or leaders to intervene to try to change things and get the dynamics back on track. And always greatly influencing how an unpredictable story unfolds, for better or worse, is organizational culture, as we'll look at in the next chapter.

CHAPTER 5

Cultures of Blame

There was once a hilarious *Saturday Night Live* segment called "Jiffy Express," about a fictional package delivery company.[1] They didn't promise on-time delivery; for that service the announcer recommended "the other guys." Instead, Jiffy offered to "take the blame" for late packages by backdating the receipt, aging the package through various means, and simulating international misrouting. Their slogan was, "When you've got no one else to blame, call us." While this was a great television skit, the unfortunate reality is that it speaks to a prevalent problem in business life: in many organizations, there is more value in finding someone to blame for being late than in getting the package mailed or delivered on time.

In far too many companies, not only individual employees' performance but the performance of the whole company is hampered by a pervasive culture of blaming. When problems occur, the first impulse is to look for someone to pin blame on. And though this may stem from a genuine belief that identifying the people to blame is the only way to solve the problem, and to prevent something like it from happening again, blaming people can leave them feeling persecuted and undermine their drive and productivity.

In my experience, if an emphasis on finding and reprimanding culprits is pervasive in a company, this tendency usually either flows from the top management down or has been established over a long period of the company's life. If you find yourself in such a corporate culture, or perhaps leading such a company, it may seem that there is no hope for progress. But even within a challenging culture, there are ways to make progress. Changing the dynamics of credit and blame can powerfully cascade up, down, and across an organization. Organizations greatly benefit by striving to learn from their mistakes and missteps, rather than succumbing to the temptation to blame individuals or groups. Indeed, too much emphasis on blaming individuals can lead to a failure to identify the true causes of problems, which may be structural—such as flaws in the systems people have to use, or which may be the results of macroeconomic or market conditions that are beyond any individual's control. Excessive blame can also come back to haunt those who dispense too much of it. Blamers might become blamees if the blame that they constantly dole out causes needless distress without yielding any benefit.

A striking example of unproductive blaming comes from psychologists Daniel Kahnemann and Amos Tversky, who told the story of some Israeli Air Force fighter pilots and their trainers.[2] Kahnemann and Tversky learned that the trainers had reached the conclusion that credit, or praise, led to worse performance, while blame led to better performance. Pilots executed better flights after they received a dressing-down, and flew worse after they had received positive feedback. To explain this pattern, the instructors had concluded that blame was effective in getting pilots to focus better, while positive feedback caused them to be cocky and overconfident. (As in the scene from the classic 1980s-era movie *Top Gun* where Kelly McGillis chides Tom Cruise for his unconventional in-air maneuvers. "I see some real genius in your flying, Maverick, but I can't say that in there.")

As a result of the instructors' conclusion about the costs of credit and the benefits of blame, it became standard procedure to withhold positive feedback and to liberally apply blame. Kahnemann and Tversky, however, reached a very different conclusion. They realized that the flight performances of the pilots actually followed a pattern called "regression to the mean," which explained why, if a pilot logged a poor flight, this "outlier" or "anomaly" would be unlikely to happen again. Chances were that his next mission would be closer to the average (better than the previous flight), regardless of the kind of feedback he had received from his superiors. Similarly, after a very good flight, the odds were that a pilot would perform more poorly, thus regressing toward the mean, on his subsequent sortie. Kahnemann and Tversky therefore learned that the trainers were off-base in thinking that they were making better pilots by skimping on credit and pouring on blame. In other words, there was an error in how the instructors assessed the impact of the credit and blame they had assigned to the pilots.

In many cases, organizational leaders underestimate the impact that credit and blame have on subordinates, but these flight instructors had actually overestimated that impact, in a kind of "superstitious" way. The knowledge of the true causes of the variation in flight quality enabled the instructors to explore new ways of teaching. Blaming the wrong factors and variables can be distracting at best, and harmful at worst.

One of the dangers of organizations' search for culprits is that it can fall prey to reaching predetermined, agenda-driven conclusions. Take the case of the 9/11 Commission. It was formed on November 27, 2002, by order of Congress and President George W. Bush with an explicit goal: "To prepare a full and complete account of the circumstances surrounding the September 11, 2001 attacks."[3] Stated another way, the government wanted to know who or what was to blame for the attacks and for the failure to prevent them. This was understandable, as the American people were enraged and wanted answers about what had happened and what should be done to ensure it wouldn't happen again. Charged with this mission, the committee, chaired by former New Jersey governor Thomas Kean, spent more than two years, and at least $9 million, preparing its final report, which totaled some 428 pages, containing sections that read like a paperback thriller. The report instantly became a bestseller upon publication.

One lesson learned, the report concludes in its final 90 pages, were that government agencies like the CIA and FBI weren't centralized enough—that their failure to communicate and share information effectively created a bureaucratic blind spot that the al Qaeda terrorists exploited to devastating effect. If the government's intelligence and antiterrorist resources had been working well, the commission reasoned, the attacks on the Pentagon and the World Trade Center towers should never have happened. And to make sure that something like it never happened again, the government needed to renew its focus on Muslim countries like Afghanistan, Pakistan, and Saudi Arabia. "The focus of our anti-terrorist strategy should not be just 'terrorism,' some generic evil," the report states. "The catastrophic threat at this moment in history is more specific. It is the threat posed by Islamic terrorism."[4]

Given that all the participants in the attack were Muslim, this all sounds reasonable, right? Not according to Richard Posner, the prominent author, blogger, and judge on the U.S. Court of Appeals for the Seventh Circuit in Chicago, who wrote a brilliant "dissent" to the 9/11 Commission Report in the *New York Times*. In this essay, Posner disputes the notion that any government can somehow protect its citizens from every surprise attack on the scale of what happened on 9/11. Choosing the attack on Pearl Harbor as an example, as well as the prior attack by al Qaeda on the World Trade Center, Posner argues that trying to blame the government for failing to anticipate such attacks may be unfair and unhelpful: "The problem isn't just that people find it extraordinarily difficult to take novel risks seriously; it is also that there is no way the government can survey the entire range of possible disasters and act to prevent each and every one of them."[5]

And yet, endeavoring to fulfil its mandate, the commission explicitly assigned blame for the failure to prevent the attacks to the structure of U.S. intelligence agencies, and proposed remedies for how the government could fix the problem. Posner argues that in so doing, the commission relied on the all-powerful tool of hindsight to identify mistakes and missed opportunities that perhaps could have prevented the attacks, even though, in all likelihood, there was little or nothing the government could have done. Additionally, in Posner's view, the commission put forth a solution that was pre-determined—the centralizing of the government's intelligence resources and appointment of a central director to lead the efforts against Islamic terrorists the world over.

By laying blame, Posner believes, the commission not only failed in its mission; it may have done something worse: created a false sense that the risk of terrorist attacks could be minimized more easily than is actually the case. "When the nation experiences a surprise attack, our instinctive reaction is not that we were surprised by a clever adversary but that we had the wrong strategies or structure and let's change them and then we'll be safe," Posner notes. "Actually, the strategies and structure weren't so bad . . . and greater dangers may be gathering of which we are unaware and haven't a clue as to how to prevent."[6] Some commentators have even argued that decentralized intelligence agencies, if appropriately interfacing with one another, might be better equipped to develop new, adaptive approaches to identifying and combating emerging threats than a single bureaucracy would. Whether it's fighting terrorism, developing innovative products, or delivering good customer service, organizations need to continuously learn in order to succeed, and reaching premature conclusions about who or what was to blame is not the optimal way to do so.

THE LEARNING ORGANIZATION

The more an organization allows or rewards a culture of finger-pointing within its walls—either of the physical or the virtual kind—the greater the likelihood that performance will suffer and that learning will fail to occur. The best organizations understand that failure and mistakes can be extremely valuable—as long as there are systems in place to ensure that individuals don't get unfairly blamed for making them, and processes that provide opportunities for the organization to learn from them.

A remarkably powerful technique that any leader, at any level, whether managing a small staff or a whole company, can use to learn vital information that might otherwise be withheld, is to give credit to those members of the organization who step forward to take blame. Consider the story of the famous German rocket scientist Wernher von Braun, who, though controversial for his role in the Nazi rocket program during World War II, was recruited immediately after the war to help lead America's fledgling space program.[7] In highly competitive organizations like NASA, where, at that time, the United States was playing catch-up to the Russians in the race to space, if something went wrong, an engineer had a strong incentive to shift blame away from himself, or even to hide his mistakes altogether. Understanding this potential trap wherein engineers might be inclined to distort or conceal the truth, von Braun saw the opportunity to change the dynamics of his organization one day when one of the U.S. Army's new ballistic missiles blew up during a test launch at Cape Canaveral, Florida.

After analyzing the data, the engineers identified what they thought was the problem and the order was given to redesign the troublesome component—a task that would put the missile's design months behind schedule. That's when a young engineer asked to speak to von Braun. Likely believing he would lose his job by doing so, the engineer bravely volunteered the information that in tightening a screw near a sensitive circuit board before the launch, he had touched off a spark exactly in the spot where the problem was thought to have occurred. But, because preflight tests had all checked out, he didn't think that anything was going to go wrong. Armed with this knowledge, von Braun canceled the redesign and pushed the team back on schedule. More important, instead of a pink slip, he sent a bottle of expensive champagne to the surprised and relieved engineer as a reward for his forthrightness.

Von Braun was sending a clear message that he would credit people for admitting mistakes instead of concealing the truth. With this powerful symbolic gesture, he helped create a culture of openness about mistakes rather than one of politics and self-protection, thereby also building a culture of continuous learning.

Indeed, one of the serious consequences for bosses—and organizations as a whole—that put too much emphasis on assigning blame is that they fail to discover avoidable potential problems, since they do not receive the critical information that might allow them to fix or prevent those problems before they become unavoidable. Whether an organization has a culture of blame or not can be a key determinant of performance at all levels.

Consider the contrasting examples of two airlines: American Airlines, which is the world's largest passenger airline yet seems to always be struggling to make money, and Southwest, an innovator in the U.S. airline industry that now boasts a market capitalization nearly four times that of its older and larger rival, in addition to posting a profit for the thirty-seventh consecutive year in January 2010.[8] In Jody Hoffer Gittell's book *The Southwest Airlines Way: Using the Power of Relationships to Achieve High Performance*, we learn that perhaps one reason for this contrasting financial performance is the two airlines' different organizational attitudes toward blame—particularly when it comes to the highly stressful and crucial task of orchestrating flight departures, a task complicated by countless variables that can cause delays. At American, Gittell found, "employees involved in the flight departure process displayed a great deal of blaming and blame avoidance toward each other for late departures and other negative outcomes." As one gate attendant told her: "Unfortunately, in the company when something goes wrong, they need to be able to pin it on someone. You should hear them fight over whose departure gets charged for the delay."[9]

At Southwest, on the other hand, Gittell found an opposite attitude, where "employees communicate about the problem itself, rather than assigning blame when difficulties occur." As one pilot told her: "We figure out the cause of the delay. We do not necessarily chastise, though sometimes that comes into play. It's a matter of working together. No finger pointing . . ."[10]

Another organization that has established a positive culture is Intuit, the Californian software company that makes products like Quicken and TurboTax. Founder Scott Cook believes that some of the company's best ideas have come from learning from mistakes or from initiatives that didn't live up to their potential. One example was a marketing campaign targeted at young people to encourage them to file their taxes online: it failed to gain any significant market share. But what the people at Intuit learned was that while young people didn't care much about filing taxes, they did care about collecting their refunds. The lessons learned from the failed campaign enabled Intuit to find more effective ways to market to younger consumers. "At Intuit, we celebrate failure," Cook has said. "Because every failure teaches something important that can be the seed for the next great idea."[11]

Organizations like Southwest and Intuit have thrived as a result of cultures that credit individuals for collaborating and blame them for finger-pointing, while organizations like American Airlines may have missed the connection between credit, blame, and performance. Mark Cannon of Vanderbilt University and Amy Edmondson of Harvard Business School consider how credit and blame is an integral aspect of organizational culture in their paper published in *Long Range Planning*—"Failing to Learn and Learning to Fail (Intelligently): How great organizations put failure to work to improve and innovate." Cannon and Edmondson note that organizations that try to use failures to learn are rare. Perhaps there are even fewer examples of organizations that actually try to fail *on purpose* as a means of speeding up the process of learning through experimentation: "We suggest that organizational learning from failure is feasible but involves skillful management of three distinct but interrelated processes: identifying failure, analyzing and discussing failure, and experimentation. Managed skillfully, these processes help managers take advantage of the lessons that failures offer, which are ignored or suppressed in most organizations."[12]

Whole organizations can be reluctant to admit weakness or failure for the same reason individuals and groups are: the potential cost in both self-esteem and social esteem. This is why so few organizations can get beyond the rhetoric of saying that they want to learn and actually create an environment conducive to experimentation and the failures that inevitably result. In most cases, organizations still hand out rewards in the form of raises, promotions, and titles to those who *avoid* failure. The downside is that by doing so, the organization misses the chance to identify—and thus avoid repeating—mistakes, or to innovate. By publicizing and even celebrating small instances of failure, organizations can prevent much bigger failures down the road. People are generally more afraid of making a mistake of commission than of omission, even though progress in organizations requires experimentation and failures of commission.

Organizational leaders can be much more effective by leveling the playing field in terms of the risks and benefits of experimenting versus doing or saying nothing. Cannon and Edmondson highlight the example of the CEO of a mechanical contracting company who pulled a $450 mistake out of the trash, and mounted it on a plaque. The point was that the CEO wanted to encourage everyone to learn from the mistake by using humor rather than punishing the person responsible for the failure, which would have only caused people to hide their mistakes in the future. The CEO described how the employee who had made the mistake was initially embarrassed, but came to take pride in the fact that the celebrated mistake saved the company a significant amount of money over time.

The key point is that organizations that fail to celebrate or even acknowledge failure also tend to miss out on the opportunity to learn. Take the reported case of resistance to learning within the U.S. Navy.[13] In July 2002, the U.S. Navy conducted a month-long war game that pitted its mighty warships against those of an unnamed hostile Persian Gulf nation. Costing upward of $250 million, it was the largest simulation of its kind ever conducted—and it had an unexpected outcome. On the second day of the exercise, the "red" forces of the enemy, commanded by a retired Marine Corps lieutenant general named Paul Van Riper, used a fleet of small, nimble speedboats to wreak massive damage on the big ships that constituted the "blue" fleet, launching a combination of cruise missile and suicide attacks. The blue fleet simply wasn't prepared for such a swarm attack and lacked the defensive capability to head it off.

The computers used to track and model the simulation estimated that Van Riper's attack would have resulted in a loss of sixteen warships and twenty thousand U.S. casualties, all in a single day. But rather than crediting Van Riper for uncovering major weaknesses in its strategy and technology, the Department of Defense stopped the simulation and called a do-over. They ran the exercise again, only this time, with rules in place that prevented Van Riper from fully utilizing his tactics. In other words, the "red" forces had to perform exactly as the navy wanted them to. Van Riper, to his credit, resigned, refusing to enable what he thought was a major mistake. The end result, to no one's surprise, was that the blue fleet prevailed over the red.

With its reliance on multi-billion-dollar aircraft carriers and complex weapons systems, the navy found it institutionally difficult to confront its vulnerability to asymmetrical warfare, even though the goal of a war game is precisely to test preparedness for such unpredictable scenarios and to simulate the aggressive actions of a hostile enemy. According to its critics, the U.S. Navy seems to have gotten stuck in the crosscurrents of organizational politics and remained overly committed to old approaches.[14] This same inertial effect is prevalent in organizations of all kinds. After all, organizational learning is stressful, difficult, and unpleasant. As MIT professor emeritus Edgar Schein has said, learning only occurs when "survival anxiety" becomes greater than "learning anxiety."[15]

A great story of just how much payoff there can be in learning to learn from failure comes from the late management expert Peter Drucker. Cannon and Edmondson mention how, in his book *Innovation and Entrepreneurship*, Drucker told the story of a German polymer lab.[16] Apparently, some of the scientists working at the lab left a Bunsen burner lit over the weekend, which overcooked the experiment they had been working on. In response, the scientists simply threw the material out. Coincidentally, an employee of the American chemical company DuPont had made the exact same mistake. Only, rather than dumping the result, he analyzed it and discovered how to synthesize what we now know as nylon. Similarly, the award-winning design firm IDEO overcomes the psychological barriers to failure and encourages its employees to fail—and learn—by adopting slogans such as "Fail often in order to succeed sooner," or, "Enlightened trial-and-error succeeds."[17]

HOPING FOR "B" BUT REWARDING "A"

When organizations focus too much on blame, they often miss the opportunity to reflect on whether there may be systemic factors that encourage people to act in ways that are counterproductive. In 1975, leadership expert Steven Kerr penned an article for the Academy of Management Executive called "On the Folly of Rewarding A, While Hoping for B," which has become a classic in the years since. Many problems in organizations are created because of faulty incentives and flawed reward systems that are set up to accomplish one thing but actually motivate people to do another, or even the opposite. As Kerr puts it: "Managers who complain about lack of motivation in their workers might do well to consider the possibility that the reward systems they have installed are paying off for behavior other than what they are seeking."[18]

Kerr describes several such examples of these mixed messages, ranging from doctors who diagnose healthy people as being sick in order to avoid potentially being blamed for miss-

ing an illness to universities that claim to prioritize professors'
teaching ability, yet only evaluate and reward them for publishing. Another example might be a high school basketball player
who excels at passing the ball, which makes his teammates better, but because his coach and the colleges that might give him
a scholarship credit only a player's ability to score, the player
passes less and shoots more—which actually hurts his team's
chances of winning.

I once consulted to a company that quantified and measured
everything the employees at the organization did using a "Six
Sigma" approach, which is a methodology that prioritizes reducing error rates through rigorous statistical analysis and process
control. Although there were some benefits of the approach,
the employees I interviewed strongly felt that their incentives
to boost their Sigma scores not only didn't fairly capture their
performance, they also didn't correlate closely enough with the
organization's true needs.

First of all, there was a temptation to "game" the system,
for example, by starting a project later so that the total time to
complete it would be shorter, or to not produce certain kinds
of products that would have been profitable but would have
lowered their Sigma scores. And second, some aspects of their
Sigma scores were out of their control. Their concerns, however, fell on deaf ears. The leader of the department was a self-
professed "evangelist" of Six Sigma, and was not open to making
any modifications of the evaluation system.

This kind of cultural problem was defined by Harvard
researcher Ronald Heifetz, who along with his coauthor and
Kennedy School colleague Marty Linsky made the helpful distinction between "technical" versus "adaptive" approaches to
organizational problems.[19] The aforementioned company was
trapped in a purely technical approach to the challenges it faced,
was a "closed system," and was not able to successfully adapt as

the world changed around it. The demoralized employees felt punished by a system that didn't reflect their true contributions, that incentivized them to work against the real interests of the organization, and that penalized them unfairly for trying to do the right thing.

On the other end of the technical-adaptive spectrum was a financial services organization that hired me to work with its human resources department to help it assess its performance appraisal system. The organization was committed to assessing all aspects of the system—from the way it was administered, to its frequency, to who participated, to the kind of criteria that were assessed. My firm and I were asked to review the entire process from start to finish, and to collect information from participants about what could make it more efficient and effective. The project helped HR make substantial improvements to each step in the system, and the fact that the changes were made was much appreciated by all of the company's employees. I have found that the best way for an organization to encourage employees to reflect and evolve is to do the same itself. This healthy organizational culture emphasized learning, and dysfunctional blame was almost entirely absent from the experience of working there.

THE SELF-BLAMING ORGANIZATION

Research has shown that there is much for companies to gain from accepting collective responsibility rather than casting blame on certain individuals or on outside factors such as market conditions. One compelling study showed that organizations that blame themselves for their poor results actually achieve higher stock prices over the long term than those that blame external factors. The researchers studied 655 annual reports issued by fourteen public companies over a twenty-one-year period spanning from 1975 to 1995. From each of those reports, they coded statements made in the letter to stockholders to count how many times companies had made self-serving statements for positive and/or negative events in the preceding year. For example, a company attributing poor results to external and uncontrollable factors might write in their annual report:

The drop in earnings this year is primarily attributable to the unexpected downturn in the domestic and international economic environment and increased international competition. These unfavorable market conditions directly contributed to a short-term slump in sales and difficulties in the introduction of several key drugs to the market. These unexpected conditions arose from federal legislation and are completely outside our control.

If the same company were to choose instead to make internal and controllable attributions for their problems, they might say something like:

The unexpected drop in earnings this year is primarily attributable to some of the strategic decisions we made last year. Decisions to acquire a new company and to push out several new drugs in international markets directly contributed to short-term decreases in earnings. As a management team, we were not fully prepared for the unfavorable conditions that emerged from both the domestic and international sectors.[20]

The researchers also controlled for outlier companies that exhibited exceptionally high or low performance trends by choosing only those companies whose performance correlated closely with that of their industry's average. They then measured the change in each firm's stock price based on how self-serving the statements in their annual reports were. The first conclusion the researchers reached was that when companies took credit for good results, there was no correlation with any change in stock price. The second conclusion the researchers reached was that when companies blamed themselves for their poor results, their stock prices were actually higher than those organizations that blamed external factors. As the researchers noted:

> We examined organizational-level causal attributions and found that these attributions influence organizational-level outcomes. We argued that attributions in annual reports represent what the organization collectively states to be the causes of positive and negative events, and people react to the organization based on these attributions.[21]

Investors want companies to assure them that they have a plan in place to overcome such external speed bumps as recessionary economies. As we saw in chapter 1, companies tend to rationalize and blame their misfortunes on events they cannot control. However, doing so might actually backfire and cause investors to worry. While it might be tempting for executives to deny responsibility and blame factors out of their control for bad results, this strategy can backfire when investors wonder: "If there are such important factors that are so far out of your control, why should we invest in your company?"

MOVING BEYOND DENIAL

Of course, organizations don't always just take an "extrapunitive" approach and blame external factors for their performance—they can also be "impunitive," and deny that anything bad happened at all. To see how this too can backfire, we can look to some recent examples from the field of medicine that show how acknowledgment of mistakes or poor performance can actually benefit an organization—in both the short and long terms.

Unlike businesses, hospitals are judged on much more than just financial results. Patients and their families judge whether a hospital and its personnel are performing well based on whether and how quickly and how fully patients recover from whatever ailment caused them to be admitted in the first place. But doctors and nurses are human, after all, and they make mistakes from time to time—such as leaving behind surgical sponges or operating on the wrong part of a patient's body. Rather than admit to making a mistake, lawyers and insurers have historically counseled both doctors and hospital administrators to adopt the practice known as "deny and defend" as a way to protect the organization from the threat of a lawsuit filed by an injured patient or his or her family.

Several hospitals, however, have taken courageous new approaches. The University of Michigan and University of Illinois health systems have been experimenting for several years with the notion of full disclosure, where they not only come clean about errors but also volunteer an apology and appropriate compensation. The result, perhaps counterintuitively, was not a surge in the number of lawsuits levied against the hospitals, as some expected. Instead, both hospitals saw a dramatic drop in the number of malpractice filings against them. In Michigan, the number of lawsuits filed in a year dropped from 262 before it began admitting responsibility to 83 after. In thirty-seven different cases where the University of Illinois admitted error, only one patient filed suit.[22]

One of the key goals, as Richard Boothman, the chief risk officer at the University of Michigan's medical center, told the *New York Times*, was not just to save the hospital money by avoiding lawsuits but to openly learn from mistakes so that they wouldn't happen again. Amy Edmondson, the Harvard Business School professor, uncovered these counterintuitive results during research she conducted on the causes of drug administration errors. What surprised Edmondson and her fellow researchers was that the most cohesive and best-led medical teams and institutions actually reported *more* errors than their counterparts. It's easy to imagine the researchers wondering why they had found that pattern, and asking themselves whether they had made some mistake in their research or analysis. But, after digging further and gathering and analyzing additional behavioral data with the help of an anthropologist, Edmondson learned the reason for the unexpected and seemingly paradoxical results: the higher-functioning teams were more willing to disclose their errors and, therefore, to learn from and avoid repeating them. Conversely, the units and hospitals that reported the fewest errors seemed to operate more out of a culture of fear, and scored worse on other independent measures of institutional performance and reputation.[23] They made more mistakes than the better hospitals—they just didn't report them.

After interviewing the nurses in the underperforming units, Edmondson recorded them describing their workplace with phrases like, "The environment is unforgiving, heads will roll," or, "You get put on trial," and complaining that the nurse manager "treats you like a two-year-old . . . and you're guilty if you make a mistake." No wonder, then, that nurses working in such a hostile environment, which insiders reportedly call the ABC model of medicine—accuse, blame, criticize—would have no incentive to disclose when they did make a mistake, or to openly discuss ways that such a mistake could be prevented in the future.

Edmondson, along with her colleagues Michael Roberto and Anita Tucker, wrote a case study for Harvard Business School that described the practices employed by Children's Hospitals and Clinics in Minneapolis. The facility's chief operating officer, Julie Morath, had instituted a program called SAFE, whose goal was, in part, to "transform the organizational culture to provide an environment conducive to discussing medical accidents in a constructive manner." Morath understood there was always inherent risk in treating sick patients; that sometimes doctors and nurses needed to improvise and even experiment to effectively care for their patients. But that wasn't a mind-set shared by all of Morath's colleagues—particularly those who believed the hospital would be setting itself up for increased litigation the more it acknowledged its mistakes and admitted when a previously untried approach had not proven successful.[24] She preferred the risks of "commission," trying something, to the near certainty of a bad outcome due to "omision," doing nothing.

Morath's ultimate goal, though, was to improve her hospital's safety record when it came to caring for its patients—something she knew could only be accomplished by openly acknowledging mistakes so they could be corrected and improved upon, by establishing "an environment in which everyone focused on learning from past mistakes, rather than 'pointing fingers' when something went wrong."[25] To help bring about this cultural shift, Morath implemented what she called "blameless reporting," which allowed anyone to anonymously communicate medical accidents without fear of reprisal. The goal, again, was to encourage everyone to debrief errors and mistakes with the goal of making sure they didn't reoccur.

At the same time, Morath wanted to improve how the hospital communicated with patients and their families when accidents did happen, with the goal of achieving the kinds of results that the hospitals in Michigan and Illinois now achieve. As an illustration of how this policy worked in practice,

Edmondson et al.'s case includes a story recounted by Brock Nelson, the hospital's CEO, about how they approached the family of a teenage boy who had received a clean bill of health from the hospital but who later died of cancer—an oversight that caused the family to sue the hospital. Even though the family lost the lawsuit, they still requested a meeting with Nelson in September 1999, which he remembered this way:

> The family had requested a meeting with me because they had a lot of ongoing issues with staff, and clearly, we had made a mistake. Before the meeting our risk manager and lawyer advised me to follow two rules: don't volunteer information and don't admit the hospital made a mistake. We met with the family, and adhered to the advice. When the meeting was over, my staff members congratulated me for conducting myself so well, because I hadn't given any information or admitted wrongdoing. I told them it was the worst meeting in my life and said I would never do that again. We stonewalled the family. It was terrible.[26]

Just months later, though, in February 2000, after Morath's program of public disclosure had been approved and implemented, Nelson took the opportunity to call the family back to the hospital, where he told them a far different story: "I met with family a second time, and this time, I told them what had happened with their son's misdiagnosis. It was very emotional. I had tears in my eyes. We were able to resolve the situation. After the meeting we hugged each other."[27]

ENCOURAGING PEOPLE TO SPEAK UP

Creating a culture in which people feel free to admit and accept responsibility for errors, or to speak up in ways that might bring punishment, is, of course, easier said than done. Most individuals are reluctant to speak up in the presence of superiors or to oppose a group consensus—particularly if they see that superior or their teammates doing something incorrectly or wrong. Amy Edmondson has also researched and written extensively about this dynamic. Edmondson and her research partner James Detert coined the term *latent voice episode* to describe the often-occurring moment of truth in a team or an organization when someone considers speaking up about an issue, problem, or an opportunity for improvement.[28]

How do you go about building a culture in which speaking up is the rule rather than the exception? Edmondson's research focuses not only on why some people speak up but also on how organizations can create the kind of structure and incentives that encourage their members to speak up before they, their superiors, or the organization as a whole collide with the proverbial iceberg. She wrote a Harvard Business School case study with Corey Hajim on the insurance giant Prudential Financial and its program, called *Safe to Say*, which illustrates a method for letting employees know that their concerns should be openly communicated.[29]

In 2002, Prudential was transforming from a mutual company owned by policy holders to a public company owned by stockholders. In making that significant shift, Art Ryan, Prudential's CEO, knew that he needed his employees to become more active in keeping the company on a straight course through a potentially perilous journey. Over the course of the transition there was a risk that critical issues would come to the attention of lower-level employees, but they might not feel comfortable informing higher-level managers about them. This was a major impetus for creating the *Safe to Say* program, whose goal was to get employees to feel empowered to speak up about work issues, regardless of how bad the news was.

The complexities and potential pitfalls of going public were only part of the reason that Ryan was driving *Safe to Say*. Ryan (who joined the company in 1994) believed that some of the problems the company had previously run into—such as unethical sales practices and compliance issues could have been avoided if middle managers had been more willing to speak up about the problems they were seeing unfold around them. And part of the reason was that Prudential, founded in 1873, had developed certain values over its long history that created a culture which became known as "old Pru." One example of this culture was that employees would often defer rather than confront each other, a practice that became known as "Pru polite." Ryan knew that to change this dynamic, he needed to find ways to get those middle managers and employees closest to the action to speak up sooner rather than later. As Bernard Winograd, the company's president of investment management, said, "In an investment organization in particular we need diversity of thought, and we need to hear from people. Saluting and following orders that are stupid is not helpful."[30]

In the end, *Safe to Say* took several years to implement. Every employee was trained about the importance of speaking up, and though progress seemed slow at first, it picked up momentum as employees began to self-select out of the organization if they were unable or unwilling to adapt to the "new Pru." Managers publicly rewarded subordinates who spoke up and saved the company from trouble. It took the entire organization's commitment to encourage employees to feel empowered to speak up.

SPEAKING UP BUT NOT BEING HEARD

Speaking up, while necessary for organizational learning and growth, is not sufficient for progress to be made if people are ignored when they do so. Consider the story of Lieutenant Edward Sims, which is recounted in detail in Michael Tushman and Charles A. O'Reilly's excellent book, *Winning Through Innovation.* Sims was a junior officer serving aboard the USS *Kentucky* in 1900, one of the navy's newly launched arsenal of battleships. At the time, victory at sea still meant outsailing or outflanking your opponent rather than blasting them sight unseen with radar-guided missiles as we would see today. Hitting a target with a gun mounted on a ship that was constantly rolling and pitching at sea was due more to luck than skill. Back then, a study conducted by the U.S. Navy found that out of 9,500 shots fired, only 121 hit their mark—and that was considered good markmanship. However, the navy, which had recently helped win the Spanish-American War, considered itself the best in the world.

But Lieutenant Sims found out that the game had changed, thanks to Admiral Percy Scott of the Royal Navy, who happened to be cruising the South China Sea aboard his flagship, HMS *Scylla,* at the same time as the *Kentucky.* Sims learned that Scott had invented something called continuous-aim firing, where a gunner could manipulate a gear that would enable him to make constant elevation adjustments in the angle of his gun. Now, rather than waiting for the ship to roll before firing, the gunner could fire away continuously. The impact went far beyond the rate of fire: given the ability to make adjustments, Scott's gunners saw their accuracy increase by a stunning 3,000 percent.

Sims knew a game-changing innovation when he saw it. He quickly implemented a similar system on board the *Kentucky.* But he didn't stop there. He then wrote an extensive report that included detailed statistics on the improved accuracy achieved by the new system, and promptly shipped it off to the Department of the Navy. As a loyal officer, he expected nothing less than to be consulted on how he could help transform and modernize the entire fleet. And yet, nothing happened. No response whatsoever. Sims was dumbfounded, but undeterred. His approach was to simply keep accumulating evidence and sending reports until someone finally took notice.

What Sims didn't realize was that the top brass back in Washington wanted nothing to do with his reports. His ideas, quite dangerously, were challenging the navy's status quo, as Paul Van Riper's would do almost exactly one hundred years later. The navy had an organizational culture that primarily recognized and rewarded a captain's bravery and skills at maneuvering. Sims, with his new technology, was challenging that paradigm and threatening vested interests. Now, the better gunner, not the better sailor, would decide naval battles. What could these top-ranking officers, veterans, and experts in naval warfare possibly learn from an upstart lieutenant stationed more than seven thousand miles away? Not much, they told themselves, especially when it came to accuracy, shooting. Besides, what did the navy need with better guns, anyway? They had just won a war and no one had any incentive to introduce such disruptive technology. Eventually, as Sims stubbornly continued to circulate his reports to whomever he could, sometimes with inflammatory language, the navy put him in his place by declaring his method "impossible," even going as far as evaluating his system in a formal test. The catch was that they conducted their experiment on dry land; quite predictably, it failed to offer the advantages conferred on a rolling ship.

Following the failed test, Sims's career was effectively over; he was labeled a "crackbrained egotist" and a "falsifier of evidence." Because he challenged the power structure in an entrenched culture, instead of being credited, he was blamed and marginalized. The story didn't end there because, fortunately, one person Sims sent his reports to, President Theodore Roosevelt, believed him. Roosevelt, who was an avid naval historian and former secretary of the navy, knew a good thing when he saw it. As a result, he quickly ushered Sims to Washington, where he promoted him to the role of inspector of target practice and charged him with refurbishing the fleet's ships with continuous-aim firing systems.[31] By what might seem like luck, Sims's career and reputation were saved from obscurity, and despite a culture that was highly resistant, the navy changed its ways and remained on the cutting edge of warfare technology. But Sims's journey from being blamed and sidelined in a distant outpost to being credited and utilized in headquarters wasn't just due to luck; it was because of great leadership, the subject of our next chapter.

CHAPTER 6

Leaders Reframe Blame

FACING BLAME

One little-known detail of the D-Day invasion—the World War II battle in which hundreds of thousands of American, British, French, and Canadian soldiers swarmed the beaches at Normandy and turned the tide of the war in favor of America and the Allies—was that Supreme Allied Commander Dwight Eisenhower had a note in his wallet on that day, June 6, 1944. Success in this sea invasion of unprecedented scale was far from certain. In fact, it was a risky strategy that could have ended in disaster. Knowing that the fate of the attack might be decided on the first day, Eisenhower had scribbled the note the evening before so that he would have prepared remarks if the invasion failed; it indicated he was ready to take personal responsibility for the nightmare scenario:

> Our landings have failed and I have withdrawn the troops. My decision to attack at this time and place was based on the best information available. The troops, the air and the Navy did all that bravery could do. If any blame or fault attaches to the attempt it is mine alone.[1]

161

Eisenhower was by no means the only military or political leader involved in the decision to launch, or the logistics of planning, the D-Day invasion. But he was in charge, and understood that he should be held accountable for the outcome, whatever it was.

When leaders openly confront the reality that they may fail, they actually increase the chances that they will succeed. On the other hand, leaders who are so afraid of potential shame and blame that they are unable to envision failure are actually more likely to fail. Great leaders always seem to find a way to credit others while blaming themselves: you might say they are more "absorbent" when it comes to blame than their "Teflon-coated" counterparts.

THE BUCK STOPS HERE

The years that followed World War II should have been good ones for Harry S. Truman, then president of the United States. Truman, who had stepped into office after the death of Franklin D. Roosevelt in April 1945, had big shoes to fill, and according to many historians, he had done that. After all, he had been at the helm of the country in its victories over Germany and Japan, and his decision to drop the world's first nuclear bombs, while horrific in their effect, also likely saved countless American and Japanese lives that would have been lost in a full-scale invasion of Japan. But just one year after accepting Emperor Hirohito's surrender, at home Truman faced a country that seemed ready to fall apart as the economy began to shift down from wartime production, turning sword factories into plowshare factories. Not only were labor unions across the country holding strikes which threatened to shut down everything from manufacturing to mass transit systems, but

Truman himself faced constant scrutiny and became a convenient scapegoat whenever anything went wrong. "Problems and decisions of every conceivable variety wound up on his desk," writes David McCullough in his *Truman* biography, "as did criticism and blame."[2]

But Truman didn't let this get the best of him. He chose instead to face the criticism and take responsibility, an approach symbolized by a 2.5- by 13-inch wooden and glass sign on his desk in the Oval Office that read: "The Buck Stops Here" (the other side said: "I'm from Missouri").[3] His friend Fred Canfil, a federal marshal who had seen a similar one on the desk of a prison warden in El Reno, Oklahoma, had given a copy of the placard to the president in October 1945. It was a derivation of a phrase that originated with the game of poker, where a marker, often a knife with a handle carved from the antler of a buck deer, designated the game's dealer. When a player wished to pass on the responsibility of dealing, he would simply *pass the buck*.

But the phrase had evolved for Truman, who happened to be an avid poker player, to mean something else: not dodging responsibility or blaming someone else for mistakes or failures. Truman could have, for example, blamed union leaders or the aftereffects of the war or the rising threat of communism for the nation's problems. Or, more easily, he simply could have laid blame on subordinates like his cabinet members or on Congress. But again and again, Truman's leadership of the country embodied the phrase on his desk in that, just as he did in the aftermath of Hiroshima and Nagasaki, he accepted full responsibility for his decisions regardless of the outcome. In one address to the National War College on December 19, 1952, Truman said: "You know, it's easy for the Monday morning quarterback to say what the coach should have done, after the game is over. But when the decision is up before you—and

on my desk I have a motto which says 'The Buck Stops Here'—
the decision has to be made." An interesting side note to this
is that Ronald Reagan reportedly also kept a plaque on that
same desk in the Oval Office, with the following inscription:
"There is no limit to what a man can do or where he can go if he
doesn't mind who gets the credit."[4] These two presidents clearly
believed that the best leaders neither finger-point at others nor
focus on getting credit for themselves.

Leaders at any level of any organization can reap great rewards
by adopting a "buck stops here" mind-set, even if, as is often
the case, the responsibility for a problem actually lies somewhere else. A client of mine, Rob, who worked at the New York
branch of a large investment bank headquartered in Europe, was
upset one year when one of his star employees, Brian, whom
Rob credited with important contributions to his group's profit-
ability, was going to get "screwed" at bonus time. For a variety
of political reasons Rob's arguments about his employee's worth
to the company went unheeded and, in Rob's view, Brian was
going to be underpaid by around $25,000. Because of his strong
conviction that Brian was not receiving fair credit for his contributions, Rob decided that he would personally make up the
shortfall out of his own pocket.

Rob's decision gratified some people and astonished the rest.
Not long after, due in no small part to the favorable visibility
and goodwill that his generosity generated among the staff, he
was promoted. As a result of his promotion, Rob got a huge
salary and bonus increase the following year, which he told me
repaid the check he wrote to Brian by a factor of fifty.

TO BLAME OR NOT TO BLAME

Some leaders come to understand the hard way how it can actually become an advantage to accept blame in the public eye. In this era of the Internet, blogs, Facebook, and Twitter, organizations must increasingly yield to customers who can organize nearly instantly with each other to protest organizational shortcomings or shenanigans. Essentially, leaders are now often forced to acknowledge their organization's role in whatever customers are mobilizing over. Andrew Grove was one of the first leaders to successfully manage in this new world. Grove, the former CEO and chairman of computer chipmaker Intel, is considered one of the most brilliant and successful corporate chieftains in history. Under his leadership between 1987 and 1997, Intel's market value increased some 4,500 percent—from $18 billion to $197 billion—making it, for a time, the world's most valuable company.

Intel continues to be a profitable and well-respected company today, helped in part by Grove's actions in addressing the Pentium Flaw Crisis of 1994.[5] Intel had placed a big bet on the success of the Pentium microprocessing chip, essentially the brains of a computer. To clear up any confusion about priorities, the rollout of the chip was called "Job 1" within the company. It was in October 1994, however, that Thomas Nicely, a mathematics professor at Lynchburg College in Virginia, informed Intel that the Pentium chip had a flaw that caused mathematical errors. Intel was aware of the flaw, which caused a rounding error in division once in every 9 billion operations, but decided that it wouldn't impact the vast majority of Pentium users. Put another way, Intel claimed a typical user could expect to run into the error once in every twenty-seven thousand *years'* worth of using a spreadsheet.

Intel did offer to consider replacing any customer's chip on a case-by-case basis, but also insisted that the burden of proof was on customers that they had a specific reason why they needed a replacement chip. Grove and his staff simply didn't believe the flaw mattered. After all, they were used to dealing with computer manufacturers, not consumers. By denying the importance of the flaw, and deflecting blame for it, they might have hoped that the whole thing would simply go away. But Nicely posted his findings on the web, which soon resulted in a wave of press coverage, with news media organizations around the world jumping on the story of "the Pentabug." And the stories had a bite, implying that Intel was knowingly shipping flawed products to its customers. Jokes also began to circulate among the late-night TV show hosts: "At Intel, quality is job 0.99989960954." Things reached a crisis point when, in mid-December, IBM, which was the dominant supplier of consumer PCs at the time, stopped shipping computers with the logo "Intel Inside." Predictably, Intel's stock began a precipitous slide.

It was then that Grove understood he had reached an "inflection point," as he called it, where the present and future reputation of his company depended on taking responsibility for the flawed chip by issuing a public apology and taking a write-off of $475 million. This was the amount needed to replace on request every one of the hundreds of thousands of chips that had been shipped into the marketplace, which were priced at $495. As he remarked in his public apology: "We are today announcing a no-questions-asked return policy on the current version of the Pentium processor. Our previous policy was to talk with users to determine whether their needs required replacement of the processor. To some people, this policy seemed arrogant and uncaring. We apologize."[6]

Grove even hired hundreds of customer service employees to deal with customer requests and to keep up with the buzz on the nascent Internet and its newsgroups to take a more proactive approach with any discussion involving Intel. (Ironically, despite all the fuss, only a small percentage of Pentium customers actually took the company up on its chip replacement offer.) By the end of the year, as a result, Intel had locked up orders of its next generation Pentium chips for 1995.

This crisis demonstrates Grove's understanding—if somewhat delayed—of how taking accountability and blame could bring substantial rewards, or at least stop further damage to the company's image. While $475 million was an enormous amount of money for the company (the equivalent of five years of advertising for the Pentium), Grove realized that without sending the message that Intel was willing to take the blame for its mistakes, he might not have had much of a company to lead before too long. The profound truth Grove had learned was that the longer a company tries to avoid taking blame upon itself, the bigger the problems it may face. As Grove would later write about that time: "I was one of the last to understand the implications of the Pentium crisis. It took a barrage of relentless criticism to make me realize that something had changed—and that we needed to adapt to the new environment."[7]

But, by then taking responsibility and initiating the necessary action to overcome the problem, Grove actually *increased* the value of his brand through his actions in the wake of the crisis. The point that the company regretted its earlier decision came through loud and clear; a joke that circulated at the time conveyed this: "Have you heard about Intel's new chip? It's called the 'Repentium.'" But the results can't be made fun of. By breaking through denial, realizing that the way he was used to operating his business needed to change, and by taking the blame both for having shipped a flawed product and for having initially denied blame by trying to minimize the importance of the flaw, Grove helped Intel regain the trust of its customers and the media.

ADMITTING FALLIBILITY

To create a culture of collaboration and responsibility, organizational leaders must set a personal example of openness, of admitting fallibility and mistakes, and of striving for continuous improvement. If we turn for some advice on this topic to MIT professor emeritus Edgar Schein, one of the fathers of the field of organizational development, we learn that great leaders are willing to turn a critical eye on themselves in the interest of building an organization capable of learning from its mistakes. As Schein told the *Harvard Business Review*:

> I would like to emphasize that unless leaders become learners themselves—unless they can acknowledge their own vulnerabilities and uncertainties—then transformational learning will never take place. When leaders become genuine learners, they set a good example and help create a psychologically safe environment for others.[8]

Schein teaches us that in the new workplace, no one, not even the CEO, is so powerful and invulnerable that he or she doesn't need to learn—which means a willingness to take risks, make mistakes in doing so, and then own the resulting blame.

This is an approach that Jim Collins advocates in his book *Good to Great.* One of the common denominators that distinguishes companies like Gillette, Kimberly-Clark, and Wells Fargo, which managed to significantly outperform their competitors over the fifteen-year period Collins studied, was that they were led by what Collins labeled "Level 5" leaders—people who blend extreme personal humility with intense professional will. These leaders, as defined by Collins, "never wanted to become larger-than-life heroes. They never aspired to be put on a pedestal or become unreachable icons. They were seemingly ordinary people quietly producing extraordinary results." At the same time, leaders who seemingly believed that they were exempt from any learning requirement went to "great lengths to preserve the image of their own track record—stepping forth to claim credit about how they were the visionary when their colleagues were not, but finding others to blame when their decisions go awry." This was the management philosophy held by those more self-focused, "bold"-type leaders of the comparison companies Collins identified whose performance was left in the dust by that of the *Good to Great* companies.[9]

While the leaders of these comparison companies pointed the finger at everything from the price of imports to the failings of their subordinates, the Level 5 leaders like Joe Cullman, the late CEO of Philip Morris, were willing to "look in the mirror" and to take blame when things didn't go well, and to "look out the window" to share credit when things did go well. When Cullman led the failed acquisition of the Seven-Up Company—which he later sold for a loss—he not only took the blame for making a bad decision, he also credited those around him who had challenged him that making the purchase might not be such a good idea. And, to emphasize the point, he set the tone by saying, as Collins cites, "I will take the responsibility for this bad decision. But we will all take responsibility for extracting the maximum learning from the tuition paid."[10]

OPEN LEADERS

A commitment to learning should entail that a leader not only opens him- or herself up to constructive criticism but actively solicits it. Hank McKinnell, the former CEO and chairman of the pharmaceutical giant Pfizer, announced that he was work-ing with an executive coach to help him become a more effec-tive leader. McKinnell, who was known to have a surplus of self-confidence, credited his coach with helping him learn to stop cutting people off with answers before they had completed their thought. He told a reporter from *BusinessWeek* that, after working with his coach, who solicited feedback from McKin-nell's staff, he learned to listen to a full question, pause, and then answer.[11]

While the term "360 Review" has gained widespread popular-ity in recent years, it is far too common to find that a company's appraisal and feedback system kicks in only at the lower tiers of its hierarchy. As Edward Lawler and Christopher Worley, pro-fessors at the University of Southern California, write in *Built to Change*, senior executives in organizations are rarely appraised and do not appraise their subordinates, which, among other negative effects, means that "employees see no senior manage-ment role modeling, and senior managers are not held account-able for their performance."[12]

Michael Dell, founder of Dell Inc., on the other hand, has made it well known that he wants to know what those within his organization think of him and his leadership. Whereas most senior leaders would prefer to give performance feedback rather than receive it, Dell has implemented an appraisal system that collects feedback from multiple levels of his organization—not just from those executives who directly report to him. But hav-ing a system in place is one thing; demonstrating a willingness to learn from the results is another. As Lawler and Worley found, Dell has used his personal appraisals as an opportunity to grow. For example, the result of one such appraisal found that mem-bers of the organization thought that Dell often acted impersonal-ly toward his employees and that he was emotionally detached from the workforce. Rather than deny or distort this finding in an effort to protect his self-esteem, Dell tackled it head-on. According to Lawler and Worley:

> Dell immediately faced his top management team and offered a frank self-critique, acknowledging that he is very shy and this can make him appear aloof and unapproachable. He vowed to change and followed up by showing a videotape of that talk to every manager in the company. Further, he put some desktop props in place to help remind him and others of the change he was committed to. For example, he put a bulldozer on this desk to remind him not to ram ideas through before testing them.[13]

Through his actions, Dell was sending a message to each and every employee of his company that yes, even I, the eponymous founder of this company, will be accountable to learn from mistakes or personal limitations and improve upon them. As Marshall Goldsmith comments, "No question one of the best ways top executives can get their leaders to improve is to work on improving themselves. Leading by example can mean a lot more than leading by public-relations hype."

Another example comes from Steve Sanger, the former CEO of food producer General Mills, who reportedly sent the following message to his employees:

> As you all know, last year my team told me that I needed to do a better job of coaching my direct reports. I just reviewed my 360-degree feedback. I have been working on becoming a better coach for the past year or so. I'm still not doing quite as well as I want, but I'm getting a lot better. My coworkers have been helping me improve. Another thing that I feel good about is the fact that my scores on "effectively responds to feedback" are so high this year.[14]

And it's not just American CEOs who embrace the power of feedback and learning. Vineet Nayar, the CEO of HCL Technologies, a global IT services company headquartered in Noida, a suburb of Delhi, India, is an exemplar of open leadership in an emerging market. Nayar told a *New York Times* reporter that a big contributor to the success of his company, which has annual revenues in the $2 billion range and employs more than fifty thousand people, is that he has both inverted the leadership hierarchy and made everything from the firm's financials to employee suggestions and annual reviews available on its intranet. That includes Nayar's own 360-degree feedback, in which some 3,800 managers participate on an anonymous basis. Nayar has taken to calling this "reverse accountability."[15]

What these executive anecdotes clearly illustrate is that just as Ed Koch, the longtime mayor of New York City, would famously walk around the city asking anyone from construction workers to Wall Street traders, "How'm I doing?," when leaders demonstrate courage by asking how they are doing and even where they may be blamed for falling short, they help create a culture of continuous learning and improvement, rather than one in which credit is taken and blame is given.

CLOSED LEADERS

Unfortunately, some leaders steadfastly fail to seek out or even accept feedback. The German-born sociologist and philosopher Theodor Adorno shared what he learned about the impact of leadership styles in his book *The Authoritarian Personality*.[16] Adorno argues that there are leaders, like the Fascists who rose to power in his country, who were prone to demand submissive and uncritical behavior from their followers toward what those leaders deemed to be appropriate social and moral norms. To assess how much of a Fascist a leader is, you could ask him or her (although I do not advise you to actually do this) to take Adorno's "F-Test," which presents statements like: "Obedience and respect for authority are the most important virtues children should learn," or, "What this country needs most, more than laws and political programs, is a few courageous, tireless, devoted leaders in whom the people can put their faith." High scorers on the test who agree with many of these assertions tend to display signs of authoritarian aggression, and the people who work in the organizations they lead learn to condemn, reject, and blame anyone who violates the social norms that have been established. With such a mindset, there are "objective" black-and-white truths that are to be believed without question; those who take a more nuanced view of the world are not to be tolerated.

In every organization, leaders must confront the temptation to take a closed approach to stifling dissent and getting everyone in line. If leaders succumb to the temptation to be authoritarian, subordinates may try to please them by following their orders to "the letter of the law," rather than verifying they have understood what the leader has requested. The paradox is that the more a subordinate tries to please an intimidating leader, the less likely it may be that he or she will end up doing what the leader actually wants done.

HOW LEADERS CAN BE MISUNDERSTOOD

Closed leaders assume that if subordinates have failed to follow through on the instructions given to them, the reason must be because the subordinate was at fault. Open leaders realize that the leader may not have been clear enough about what was expected.

Some of the most well-known quotations in our culture were never actually said. The words "Play it again, Sam," for example, are never actually spoken in *Casablanca*. "Houston, we have a problem," which has become part of our cultural lexicon to communicate a dangerous situation, wasn't what the astronauts aboard Apollo 13 actually said. (What Commander James Lovell said was, "Houston, *we've had* a problem.") The truth is that we often hear, or remember hearing, things that were never actually said. I remember when I learned that a phrase that I had often used, "for all intensive purposes" was actually "for all intents and purposes." This kind of mishearing is known as a *mondegreen*, which is defined as the mishearing or misinterpretation of a phrase—typically a line in a poem or a lyric in a song—due to near homophony, in a way that yields a new meaning. It was Sylvia Wright, an American writer, who coined the term in 1954 in an essay, "The Death of Lady Mondegreen."

Wright tells about how in hearing the seventeenth-century ballad "The Bonnie Earl O' Murray" as a child, she had misheard the final line, which is "And laid him on the green," as "Lady Mondegreen." She adds: "The point about what I shall hereafter call mondegreens, since no one else has thought up a word for them, is that they are better than the original."[17] In other words, when we mishear something, we begin to construct new meanings. Rarely does a day pass in an organization without some kind of *mondegreen* arising. Ironically, the more leaders blame subordinates for misunderstanding things, the less likely the subordinates may be to understand what it is the leader wants.

It's helpful for leaders to realize that what they are saying doesn't always get heard or understood—often because they overestimate how clearly they are communicating. I once attended a leadership development program where the instructor took us through an interesting exercise. She asked us to pair off, and then tap out a song on the table, asking our partners to discern what we were tapping. It was amazing to see how "Happy Birthday" or "The Star-Spangled Banner" seemed so clearly sounded out by the tapper, and yet was so hard to identify for the listener. Of course, misunderstandings can occur any time two or more people are interacting with one another, but the dynamics of credit and blame can make communication between leaders and their followers even more problematic.

Consider the following examples of how communication gaps can open up between leaders and their staffs. Winston Churchill once asked his staff to schedule a meeting with someone he wanted to see, tersely telling them to "bring me Berlin."[18] In Churchill's mind, "Berlin" was clearly the philosopher Isaiah Berlin. "Berlin" subsequently arrived at 10 Downing Street, and Churchill, curious about the intellectual's latest thinking, asked him what he was working on. When the reply was, "A song called 'White Christmas,'" Churchill realized that his staff had brought him Irving Berlin instead of Isaiah. A similar misunderstanding occurred when J. Edgar Hoover was reviewing a classified document. Hoover had given orders that all FBI written material was to have standard, wide margins. But the memo's writer had narrowed the standard margins so that he could cram in all he had to say into the allotted page limit, making it difficult to read. Hoover scribbled a reply that simply said: "Watch the borders!," which he clipped to the report and passed along to his secretary. When his staff saw the note, however, they thought they had just received an order from Hoover to monitor the nation's borders. As a result, they sent FBI agents from around the country to drop what they were doing and head to the borders with Canada and Mexico, even though no one understood what the borders might have to do with the case in question.[19]

To make sure they actually get what they want, leaders must be conscious of what they actually say, be aware that what they ask for might be interpreted differently than intended, and make clear that they will credit people for requesting clarification rather than blaming them for doing so. As clichéd as it may sound, "active listening," wherein a leader asks subordinates what they have heard and understood, is the best antidote to organizational mondegreens. I once worked with an executive coaching client, Murray, on a memo he was sending out, and we emailed it back and forth eight times before we agreed that he had clearly gotten his point across. We all have a hard time realizing how others are going to receive the messages we are sending. Some leaders, though, have a much harder time than others. Mindful leaders don't reflexively blame subordinates for misunderstanding; instead, they endeavor to understand their own role in making things clearer, and even blame themselves when they haven't done enough to make sure that the messages they send are the messages that get received.

FOSTERING LEARNING

The stance a leader takes with respect to blame is also a key determinant in whether a team, department, or whole organization will have a culture of learning from mistakes. Consider the following story about Thomas Watson, Jr., the former president of IBM, as told by Paul B. Carroll and Chunka Mui in their *Billion-Dollar Lessons*. Watson, who headed up IBM throughout the 1960s, summoned an executive to his office following a disastrous failed venture that had cost the firm some $10 million. As the executive walked into his office, Watson asked him: "Do you know why I called you here?" Knowing of Watson's legendary temper, the executive replied: "I assume you're going to

fire me." "Fire you?" Watson said. "I just spent $10 million edu-
cating you. I just want to be sure you learned the right lessons."[20]

Fostering a learning organization has also always been of
particular interest to Elbert "Burt" Rutan, the CEO of Scaled
Composites, a high-tech company with 125 employees based
in Mojave, California. Following in the footsteps of Wernher
von Braun, Rutan's company became the first private business to
send human beings into outer space, on the forty-seventh anni-
versary of the launch of Sputnik 1. The feat earned Rutan and
his team the Ansari X-Prize, which included $10 million in cash.
But it wasn't just a passion for the "race to space" that Rutan had
in common with his role model; it was an understanding that
in order to evolve, his company needed to admit and learn from
mistakes before they cost people their lives. As David Freedman
points out in his profile of Rutan, whom *Inc.* magazine named
its 2004 Entrepreneur of the Year:

> Rutan makes sure that when people at Scaled Composites point
> out their own mistakes, they're applauded rather than repri-
> manded. And instead of extensively analyzing a design before
> building it, a notion that's axiomatic in the aerospace industry,
> Rutan pushes his people to get a first version built quickly, test
> it, and fix it. Says [Chief Engineer Matthew Gionta]: "Testing
> leads to failure, and failure leads to understanding."[21]

NO DOUBLE STANDARDS

Humility is one of the most powerful traits of a truly great leader,
which allows leaders to set an example by holding themselves to
the very same set of standards they hold others to.

When leaders do this, they inspire commitment, cohesion,
and loyalty. The standards for credit and blame that credible

leaders create then positively influence their entire organizations. Unfortunately, many leaders hold themselves to different standards than others, or do not personally exemplify the behaviors or values that they are asking others to demonstrate. The power of setting a better example should not be underestimated.

In January 2007, Richard Knoebel was driving on his daily commute from his home to his office in downtown Kewaskum, Wisconsin, when a nearby truck momentarily distracted him. In that instant as he looked to his right, he missed the fact that on the other side of the street, a school bus had stopped, its light flashing and its big red stop sign extended. Fortunately for Knoebel, there was no police officer present to ticket him—perhaps because Knoebel was actually the police chief of his small town, which is about a fifty-mile drive from Milwaukee. But Knoebel decided to issue *himself* a ticket, anyway. Not only did that ticket come with a $235 fine, it added four points to his license. "When we get someone for not stopping for a flashing school bus we give them a citation," Knoebel told a local news team after word of his self-imposed fine got around town. "So I shouldn't be any different."[22]

Knoebel's story became something of a national sensation because it seemed so out of the ordinary; but it actually demonstrates a powerful principle for leaders. Knoebel intuitively understood the power of "leading by example," and was willing to hold himself accountable for his actions even though he could have easily kept on driving that January day and never looked back. Another example of a leader who held himself to the same standard as everyone else in his organization is Kent Kresa, the former head of aerospace contractor Northrop Grumman, who, according to Marshall Goldsmith, led a turnaround at his troubled company—growing it from near bankruptcy to a thriving company with some $28 billion in revenue—through leading by example:

[Kresa] communicated clear expectations for ethics, values and behavior. He made sure that he was evaluated by the same standards that he set for everyone else. He consistently reached out to coworkers. He didn't just work to develop his leaders—he created an environment in which the company's leaders were working to develop him.[23]

Another leader who understands the value of leading by example is Ursula Burns, CEO of the Xerox Corporation. Burns, who became the first African-American woman to lead a large public corporation, has worked for the company for more than thirty years. During that time she began to climb the corporate ladder because of her willingness to take a series of executive assistant jobs that provided access to the company's top leaders, as well as the chance to demonstrate her talents and personality to them and the company's board of directors.

And what those leaders learned about Burns over the years is that she was always willing to courageously "speak up" to her superiors and teammates—something that got her promoted rather than fired. At the same time, she was open to feedback and advice—always willing to listen and to take steps to improve her skills. Part of what she learned on her journey to the top was how to strategically use credit to build alliances and accountability. One insight she has shared comes from a suggestion she received from former Xerox president Paul Allaire, who told her to give people "credit for ideas that they didn't have, but you sold to them, to give them ownership." She is also very vocal about encouraging Xerox employees to "decide" and to "do things"—a nod to the fact she wants them to take risks to help the company grow rather than worry about being blamed for making mistakes.[24]

But perhaps the most impressive trait Burns has demonstrated during her tenure at the top has been her humility—an attribute that would merit the admiration of Jim Collins. After being named CEO, Burns received global attention, but didn't get carried away by all the credit she was personally receiving. She preferred that the focus be shifted from herself and back to the company. As a reporter for the *New York Times* quotes:

> "The accolades that I get for doing absolutely nothing are amazing—I've been named to every list, literally, since I became the C.E.O.," Ms. Burns says. Apart from working on the Affiliated Computer acquisition, she asks, "What have I done? In the first 30 days, I was named to a list of the most impressive XYZ. The accolades are good for five minutes, but then it takes kind of a shine off the real story. The real story is not Ursula Burns. I just happen to be the person standing up at this point representing Xerox."[25]

Although Burns leads one of the biggest corporations in the world, her neighbors see her shopping for groceries near her home in Norwalk, Connecticut. When she arrives on the tarmac, returning from a business trip, she drives her own car home. She takes her role as CEO very seriously and knows that she sets an example for her entire organization with everything she does or does not do.

One of the most powerful ways in which humility assists in good leadership is in allowing us not only to be receptive to criticism from those below us in an organization but to credit subordinates who blame us for the right reasons. In his book *Inviting Disaster*, James Chiles tells the story of how, in the fall of 1968, astronaut Wally Schirra dropped in to have a firsthand look at Apollo 7, which he would soon ride to become the first human to fly in space three times. A veteran pilot, Schirra was in the habit of verifying the condition of his craft before flying it, so he climbed into the command module to have a look around while doing his best not to touch anything. In ducking down to squeeze through a hatch, however, he inadvertently knelt on a bundle of wires. A female worker who happened to notice what happened instantly got very angry and slapped Schirra across the face. "Don't you dare touch those wires," she said. "Don't you know we lost three men?"

The three men she was referring to were Gus Grissom, Ed White, and Roger Chaffee, who were killed in January 1967 when a launch pad fire destroyed Apollo 1. Schirra might have been angry at being slapped, and could have tried to use his position to have her fired on the spot. As soon as the worker realized who he was, she was mortified and became very apologetic. But rather than act reflexively or take the slap personally, Schirra assured her: "I want people like you working on this spacecraft." Schirra chose to convey his appreciation for the woman's dedication and passion to protect the astronauts. He credited her for blaming him, knowing that he had made a mistake and that her concern was actually for his own safety.[26]

Sometimes we react much too emotionally when others blame us. However, we should always try to stop the impulse to overreact and instead pause to process the reasons why they are doing so. Great leaders communicate—as Schirra did—the message that any action that helps achieve the mission is worthy of credit, and any action that endangers the mission merits blame, regardless of the status or rank of the person performing either type of action.

If we look at the effects of the actions of leaders like Dwight Eisenhower, Thomas Watson, and Ursula Burns, we see that they used symbolic, substantive, and structural methods to change the potentially destructive dynamics of blame in their organizations. Great leaders send clear signals when it comes to rewarding cooperation and contributions to the common good; they hold themselves accountable to the same standards as everyone else, and solicit feedback and accept blame in order to raise their game. By crediting people who are willing to confess their mistakes, such transformational leaders help create and sustain adaptive cultures. At the same time, these leaders can create disincentives for individuals to engage in selfish behavior and provide incentives for them to fix rather than blame.

In underperforming organizational cultures, where leaders fail to set an example, individuals learn that it is in their interest to blame rather than fix. In great organizations, where leaders mindfully use and improve the dynamics of credit and blame to constantly cultivate collaboration, openness, and a sense of responsibility, every individual, group, and department has an incentive to focus on the tasks at hand and achieve organizational goals rather than expending valuable time, energy, and resources in trying to avoid blame or to rationalize why the goals were not achieved.

CHAPTER 7

Practical Approaches

We face the challenge of coping with the blame game at work in many different ways. Perhaps you work for a boss who is always looking to pin blame on you, or your whole team has become so caught up in finger-pointing that the environment at the office has become toxic. Maybe one of your teammates is constantly taking credit that really should go to you. Or maybe you are a boss yourself, and are dealing with a team in which everyone wastes your time by blaming each other instead of fixing problems.

I hope that the descriptions and explanations I've offered about common problems in the workplace will help inform your strategies for addressing whatever issues you may be facing—whether as subordinate, peer, or boss. I can't offer, however, a comprehensive playbook for how to deal with credit and blame issues. As we've seen, there is so much complexity, and so many variables involved in any given workplace problem, that it is simply not possible to come up with "one size fits all" strategies. But in this last chapter, I will offer several general ideas as to how individuals and leaders at any level can avoid common pitfalls, defuse the tensions, and intervene to prevent or fix destructive dynamics that can so easily take hold.

FOR INDIVIDUALS
TAKING A STEP BACK

If you find yourself dealing with a particular "blame-thrower" or an egregious real credit-grabber, whether it's your boss or a co-worker, the first thing to do is try to get some perspective on the problem—to step back and dial down the emotion you're feeling—by systematically reflecting on the wide range of possible influences on that person's behavior that we've examined in this book. Remind yourself, for one thing, that we all have the natural tendency to cast blame, which is bred into us to some extent, and that doing so can be a largely subconscious process. Then reflect on how that person may have been influenced to behave in that way by his or her upbringing. Maybe her approach to managing is largely a result of having grown up in a highly punitive family, or is because of her cultural socialization.

It's almost never going to be the case that you'll be able to discover precisely what background factors might have shaped that person's approach to credit and blame; after all, we can't exactly ask our colleagues intrusive questions about their upbringing, families, or cultural background. But just keeping present in our minds the fact that such influences can be so powerful tends to be very helpful empowering in understanding and learning to cope with their behavior. The same is true for considering how a person's fundamental personality type and particular combination of personality dimensions and subfactors may be at work. This is not to say that we should give people a pass on bad behavior just because "their personality makes them do it." But given the fact that at work we are usually quite constrained in terms of how directly we can confront people about their behavior toward us—especially if that person is our boss or another higher-up—we have to first understand the complexities of "why" they are acting as they do before we can formulate a nuanced and effective strategy for "how" we can endeavor to positively influence them.

BE STRATEGIC ABOUT CREDIT AND BLAME FOR YOURSELF AND OTHERS

Even if you find yourself working for a difficult boss, there are productive ways to behave, and unproductive ways, and it's easy to make a bad situation worse. As the examples of Pria and Robert Kearns showed, people often suboptimize how they go about seeking credit or avoiding blame. It's hard, but helpful, to avoid the temptation to fight for credit and recognition to a self-defeating extent, or to trade your substantive interests for symbolic recognition. You need to make sure you don't win the battle but lose the war.

There may be a difference between the *true* picture of credit and blame and the *strategic* picture of credit and blame. While it's never a good idea to unfairly blame others, it can sometimes be helpful to share more credit than you perceive that others deserve. As we've explored, most of us overestimate our own contributions and underestimate others', like an optical illusion in which two lines of identical length appear to be different. Knowing this, you can err on the side of sharing slightly more credit than you are inclined to about something that you genuinely believe to be creditworthy, since it's not in your interest to "fake" giving credit to others. It's likely that the other person deserves more credit than we are inclined to give him; and even if he doesn't, sharing more credit with him may just be the first positive move that encourages him to reciprocate by sharing more credit with us. Just as there can be financial "credit crunches" that slow down the economy, there can be credit crises in the workplace that undermine trust and collaboration. No matter what level you work at, taking a risk and sharing more with others might help get the frozen credit flowing again.

If you share more credit, and still do not feel that others are reciprocating, it's helpful to consider first of all whether you are correct in your determination, and if so, to consider why the other person might be withholding credit before you begin to fight for what you believe to be your due. One of the easiest ways to make the dynamics of credit and blame worse is to push too hard, too fast. Even if you have validated with others that your perceptions of unfair dynamics are accurate, be careful about the timing and the way in which you decide to "speak truth to power." If you push back too hard on a boss or colleague or team, you may end up making them more rigid and defensive. A more subtle long-term approach may not only be more effective; it may also be safer and reduce the possibility that you will be scapegoated by your team, resented by your colleagues, or persecuted by your boss. The stories of Genna and Dana both show how taking a more subtle and patient approach can lead to a successful outcome. Sometimes the most strategic thing you can do is to simply give a situation time to unfold.

FOCUS ON WHAT YOU *CAN* DO

As I've emphasized, we all have much more power to change how we perceive situations, and what we do, than we have over how others perceive things, or what they do. Therefore, self-awareness is the foundational ingredient of being able to change a situation; or, in unfortunate cases where the situation can't be changed, of helping us to recognize that we need to abandon that situation.

Workplace relationships—particularly those between bosses and subordinates, or direct peers—are often quite emotionally complex, and, given the right situation and interpersonal chemistry, tensions at work can cause any of us to reenact counter-productive patterns from our earlier lives, or even (especially in highly stressful situations) to regress to more primitive stages of human evolution. Knowing your personal history and under-standing your triggers is the most reliable way to avoid the traps of the blame game.

People who have successful careers often become historians of their own career trajectory, and can tell the "story" of their success in a compelling way that includes the whys of how their career has unfolded. Developing this kind of awareness is an important tool in career advancement. Try to remember that under pressure, you might face the danger of reverting to old patterns that could work against your career success. Each of us faces the temptation to internalize too much credit and to exter-nalize too much blame. Everyone develops credit and blame "habits" over the course of their lives and careers, and these hab-its can be good or bad. As we've seen, people who get stuck in the habit of chronically blaming others are more likely to derail their careers or the companies they lead.

In addition to keeping your personal "story" in mind, analyz-ing your own personality is often very useful for gaining a new perspective on how you are likely to deal with credit and blame problems. Figuring out where you score on the Big Five person-ality dimensions is a good way to begin considering the different elements of your personality and how they interact with each other to help explain your workplace preferences and behaviors. These personality dimensions can also shed light on how you interact with others, and can provide a perspective on why some workplace relationships are enjoyable and productive while oth-ers are unpleasant and trying.

For a free online test of the Big Five dimensions and subfac-tors described in chapter 3, you can go to www.personal.psu .edu/j5j/IPIP/ipipneo120.htm.

"KNOW THY RISK FACTORS"

In addition to learning about the basic building blocks of your personality, it's also helpful to assess which of the dysfunctional "types" you may be at risk for, or may be perceived as demonstrating. The Credit and Blame Type Assessment, which I developed with Paul Connolly in consultation with Robert Hogan and market in partnership with Performance Programs, Inc. can be accessed at www.performanceprograms.com/blamegame. After you fill out the questions for this assessment, you will receive a customized report that lists a "percentile score" of how likely you are to be perceived as displaying each of the eleven dysfunctional personality types described in chapter 3.

Keep in mind that if you are in a certain "state" at your job, it can influence the likelihood that you will be tempted to respond to workplace pressures in a dysfunctional way. As trite as it may sound, getting enough sleep and exercise, eating right, and leading a balanced and fulfilling life outside of work can greatly enhance our ability to deal with the inevitable trials and tribulations inside the workplace.

Try to work with bosses and peers, and in teams and organizations, that bring out the best in you, in order to minimize the risk that you will find yourself in a situation that will be demoralizing and in which you may act dysfunctionally. If you come to believe over time that your boss is exhibiting some of the attributes of the dysfunctional types described in chapter 3, you can still learn from the experience not only about your career preferences but about what kinds of bosses to avoid going forward. Here is a sample list—by no means mutually exclusive or exhaustive—of what you might learn about yourself and your risk factors from the experience of working for different kinds of bosses:

Extrapunitive types:

Excitable—or Volatile Guardian: Working for such a person is particularly challenging for anyone who likes to work in a stable, predictable environment.

Cautious—or Sensitive Retirer: Anyone who requires close collaboration with, and public recognition from, their supervisor should avoid this kind of boss.

Skeptical—or Wary Watcher: If having a trusting and open relationship with your boss and a strong network across the organization is important to you, avoid skeptical bosses.

Leisurely—or Rationalizing Blamer: If it's important to you that your boss has a good relationship with, and support from, his or her superiors, it's generally better to steer clear of leisurely bosses.

Impunitive types:

Bold—or Big Person on Campus: Anyone who needs warmth and support from a boss or manager should avoid this kind of manager, who is likely to be highly self-interested and self-involved.

Mischievous—or High Wire Walker: Anyone who requires a boss who demonstrates a high degree of trustworthiness and integrity should avoid this kind of manager at almost any cost.

Reserved—or Indifferent Daydreamer: People who want team spirit under a boss who is "present" and provides positive feedback may be particularly vulnerable to disappointment if they work for a reserved boss.

Colorful—or Thespian: If drama in life or work makes you uncomfortable, it's a good idea to audition other bosses instead of taking a role under the direction of a "thespian," since people who work for this kind of boss will likely experience interludes of terrifying theatrics.

Imaginative—or Assertive Daydreamer: If you want a warm, connected, and "present" boss, this type is not likely to be a good fit for you, since he will live mainly in his own head.

Intropunitive types:

Diligent—or Micromanager: If you bristle at an overbearing, command-and-control management style, then probably the last kind of boss you want would be a "diligent" type.

Dutiful—or Martyr: If you want a boss who is comfortable taking credit for him- or herself and his or her team, a dutiful boss will likely make you feel undercredited and underappreciated by the rest of the organization.

FIGHT THE FUNDAMENTAL ATTRIBUTION ERROR

Keep in mind that it's easy to make the fundamental attribution error (see page 42) when evaluating why someone seems to be unfairly blaming us, failing to give us due credit, or grabbing credit from us. Think about "walking a mile in their moccasins," and take their own constraints into account before reaching a conclusion about their intentions or capabilities. Remember that there's always an inferential and interpretive leap between what someone does in a given situation and his or her capabilities or character. It's helpful to observe how different individuals act similarly in some situations, and also how those same individuals may act differently in other situations. In other words, situations can cause different people to act the same way or can cause the same people to act in different ways. You will likely see that situational factors not only play a large part in behavior in general; they also affect how credit and blame are given and received. In addition to considering the person's situation, it's important to keep his or her role in mind when you evaluate their behavior or performance. In all likelihood, situational influences and the person's role will explain at least as much of their behavior, if not more, as personality will.

FIGHT THE ULTIMATE ATTRIBUTION ERROR

In addition to all of us being susceptible to overattributing behavior to a person's disposition rather than to the situation in which he or she is working, we have all been hardwired to commit the ultimate attribution error (see page 117) by interpreting a person's behavior based on his or her group membership. Because of unconscious associations we all have between someone's group membership and various positive or negative attributes, we are likely to assign credit and blame in a manner congruent with these biases. Additionally, it's very easy to hold one's own group to a different standard than other groups, and to demonstrate a "group-serving bias" for one's group which is the equivalent of a "self-serving bias" for oneself. However tempting it may be, do not rush to judgment about the capabilities, intentions, or trustworthiness of people solely based on their group identification.

As we saw in chapter 2, the Implicit Associations Test can help you gauge your unconscious stereotypes and biases against members of different groups. To take this test for free online, go to https://implicit.harvard.edu/implicit/demo/. Once aware of any biases you may be prone to, you can work to correct them as you go about evaluating people and their performance.

START WITH POSITIVE EXPECTATIONS AND GIVE PEOPLE THE BENEFIT OF THE DOUBT

As in the Prisoner's Dilemma scenario and the optimal "tit-for-tat" strategy, it's best to start off with positive expectations, and to give people the benefit of the doubt. By initiating workplace relationships with positive expectations, you increase the likelihood that others will reciprocate with positive behaviors. Although there may be some risk to assuming the best about others, over the long run it is a better strategy than assuming the worst, because of the dynamics of self-fulfilling prophecies that we have explored.

Even in conflict situations, try to avoid escalating negative cycles of blame, and instead attempt to create positive, self-fulfilling cycles of learning and growth. Because of the dynamics of self-fulfilling prophecies and projective identification, in most cases it makes better sense to try a positive approach than a negative one, even after a conflict has begun to brew. Using the "stick" of blame to try to change people's behavior is generally not as effective as the "carrot" of credit. Positive reinforcement is a much better influence strategy than punishment. So, even in a situation with a difficult colleague or boss, try to find something that person is doing that you appreciate or admire, and let him know, in a genuine way, that you credit his talents. Confirming people's hopes about themselves is a far better influence strategy than confirming their fears.

ARTICULATE THE ISSUES

In *Your Brain at Work*, leadership consultant and coach David Rock describes neurological research that has shown that different parts of the brain are involved in having emotional experiences versus telling a story or narrative about those experiences.[1] Rock recommends that it's often helpful, in an emotional workplace situation, to try to label an experience in order to gain perspective and distance, as opposed to simply acting based on reflex and impulse. In my work, I have also found that it can be very beneficial when clients go through the exercise of describing in words highly charged situations involving credit and blame. By talking about a situation, and describing it, people are already beginning to gain perspective and distance. Therefore, whenever you encounter a highly emotional or challenging situation involving credit and blame, it's always a good idea to try to put your experience into words—whether to a friend outside of work, your partner or spouse, or a trusted colleague.

LOOK FOR A PATTERN

It's also helpful in getting perspective to try to describe how your present experience relates to other experiences you've had in the past. Ask yourself if you've run into the same problem, or set of problems, before—not for the purpose of blaming yourself for the current situation, but in order to understand your role in whatever might be going on. Even if what is happening is out of your control, it's useful to understand how your reactions can be contextualized in the broader perspective of your life and career. We all know people who fall back into the same patterns wherever they go: who keep dating the wrong people, getting into the same fixes, or repeating the same complaints. They meet the new boss and, lo and behold, she's the same as the old boss; but actually the storyteller is the only common denominator. While it's easy to see how friends and family keep making the same mistakes and reenacting the same scripts over and over again, it's much more difficult to see how we do this ourselves. As a starting point, try thinking about bosses and colleagues you most enjoyed working with. What did these experiences have in common? Also, think about situations where the chemistry was wrong for you and consider why things didn't work out.

GET FEEDBACK, VALIDATE PERCEPTIONS

In addition to reflecting on your career experiences, it's helpful to get feedback from colleagues, family, friends, and advisers to learn how they have seen credit and blame play out in your work life, for better or worse. How do they see your story? What suggestions do they have for you? How much of the chemistry and dynamics were due to the *people* you were working with, and how much to the *situation* you and they were working in? Or how much of your experience was due to your traits and personality, and how much to the state you were in at that point in your career? If you were to go back to that same workplace situation now, might the plot unfold in a different way?

Solicit "360-degree feedback" from others to benchmark how you evaluate your own performance against how others evaluate it. Learn from others' perceptions and perspectives even if you don't agree with them. Try to see what you are doing—or not doing—from different points of view so you can reevaluate and improve your performance. To take a "Credit and Blame 360" to solicit feedback from people whom you work with about how you attribute credit and blame, you can access an online 360 survey that I developed and market in partnership with EchoSpan, Inc: www.echospan.com/blamegame.

Another online tool for gathering feedback is Rypple.com, which is a self-directed informal online performance appraisal tool. You can set up a free account at rypple.com. You enter in the questions that you would like people you work with to answer about you. Each of your "raters" then gets a survey via email and you receive an anonymous report of how they responded. Questions you may want to ask could include:

- How do I come across in the ways I assign credit and blame?
- Do I hold myself to the same high standards that I hold others to?
- Do I claim more credit than I am due?
- Am I fair in the amount of credit I share with others?
- When things go wrong, do I acknowledge my own role in the disappointing results?
- Do I help reinforce a constructive culture of sharing credit and accepting blame?
- Am I focused more on problem solving than on finger-pointing?
- Am I willing to speak truth to power even when doing so creates the risk that I will be blamed?
- Do I encourage people to speak up and push back?

DEVELOP YOUR KNOWLEDGE, SKILLS, AND NETWORKS

One last point about how you can contend with the problems you might run into at work is that the more highly functioning you are and the more indispensable you make yourself to your organization, the less likely it is that you will become a victim of undue blaming. If you develop your knowledge, skills, and professional network to the point where your boss and your organization come to view you as a "flight risk," you may find that the flow of credit toward you becomes more favorable, even if your boss hasn't undergone some magical transformation. Market conditions also matter. If you were a Java programmer in the late 1990s during the dot-com boom, Internet start-ups didn't care if you bathed or shaved, and would pretty much give you anything you wanted if you agreed to work for them. When I worked with some Internet companies during this time, most Java programmers could do no wrong, since their bosses and companies were so afraid of losing them. A few years later, after the dot-com bust, the Java programmers who didn't lose their jobs experienced a lot less credit and much more blame at work each day. Bosses who had been super-friendly and considerate suddenly became much less friendly and much more critical because of the tougher conditions in which everyone was working.

A generally effective way to make sure that you get the credit you're due and to prevent unfair blame from getting heaped on you is to develop internal and external business networks. A boss who denies you credit and unfairly blames you may change her tune when she realizes that others both inside and outside the organization recognize your talents. If you build a robust network, you are more likely to be offered other jobs, both inside and outside the company, and even the most credit-hogging and blame-dumping boss will not want to be viewed as out of step with others in the organization, or to be blamed for being the reason why a talented, hard-to-replace employee left the organization.

FOR ORGANIZATIONAL LEADERS
BE A BLAME-SAVVY BOSS

In managing others, if you are quick to judge, self-serving, and biased toward certain people in the credit and blame you assign, the cohesion of your team and the loyalty they feel toward you will suffer. On the other hand, if you are thoughtful, self-critical, and fair in assigning credit and blame, you are likely to inspire deep appreciation and commitment from your staff. By setting the right example, you can instill in them an ethic of mutual support and collaborative problem solving, rather than one of defensiveness and finger-pointing.

One way to set a positive example is to hold yourself to the same high standards that you hold others to, giving yourself a metaphorical traffic ticket, as Richard Knoebel did, if you do something that you find blameworthy. Clearly convey that you use the same criteria and standards for yourself as you use to evaluate others, letting people know that the same rules and standards apply to everyone. If your team perceives that you use different standards for yourself, they will get the message that credit and blame are assigned based on "power" instead of "truth"; and if they absorb this message, they will stop speaking truth to power, potentially failing to provide you with critical information.

Another way to set a positive example is to share credit and take blame in a manner that entails some vulnerability and risk. When things go well, it's tempting to collect the credit, and when things go wrong, to deny blame or blame situations or other people. However, great bosses and leaders, as Jim Collins and others have described, take care to credit other people for positive outcomes and blame themselves for negative ones. By being willing to make themselves open, great leaders encourage their organizations to take the calculated risks, experiment and learn, despite the vulnerability that results when old approaches are set aside and new approaches tried.

TAKE AN OPEN, ADAPTIVE APPROACH

As Edgar Schein said, you can't be a transformational leader if you are not willing to transform yourself: only if leaders themselves take a learning approach can they hope to lead an organization successfully. As a leader, one of the most important ways to take a learning approach is to not reflexively blame your staff. Even in situations where it seems clear that your team has made errors of omission or commission, look before you blame. While your first hypothesis may be that your staff messed up, test this assumption before embracing it as a conclusion. Perhaps your instructions were unclear or your expectations unreasonable, or maybe circumstances made it impossible for your instructions to be followed. It's possible they didn't have the resources, information, or organizational support they needed. Or your people might have done what you asked if you hadn't also asked them to do other, additional work at the same time.

Asking whether you yourself may have directly or indirectly added to your staff's challenges in achieving the goal is also helpful. Even if it turns out that the mistake was their error alone, conveying that you are willing to be self-critical and consider your own role is likely to inspire confidence and loyalty. If, on the other hand, they feel like you always blame them without considering other factors in general, or your own role specifically, they are likely to feel helpless, demotivated, and resentful.

Whenever giving feedback, whether formal or informal, inside the company's review process or outside it, give employees the opportunity to share with you how they think you or the organization could be more supportive as they endeavor to achieve the goals you set for and with them. Even if you are unwilling or unable to provide exactly the resources or support they request, being open to their point of view will likely be appreciated.

FOCUS ON THE FUTURE INSTEAD OF THE PAST

While feedback and understanding the past can be very helpful at times, sometimes the best course of action is to not argue about the past, but instead to focus on the future. However, this can be hard to do, since most bosses and organizations tend to give feedback about past behavior and performance. Not only are we encouraged to request feedback from our bosses and co-workers, but there is an innate desire within each of us to give feedback. It's as if we are driven to constantly dig up and rehash the past—particularly when it comes to someone else's flawed actions or behavior. All too often, our notion of feedback is something along the lines of: "Here's what you did wrong" or "You didn't succeed because . . ."

When someone succeeds at something, though, they are almost never called into the boss's office to receive feedback on how or why they were so successful. Feedback, it seems, is too often just another way of recasting blame, since it is generally used to show how someone could have done something differently or better. But, as the saying goes, hindsight is always twenty/twenty vision. Clearly, there is much to be learned from past events, but the way we frame the lessons can help us both receive and internalize them far more effectively.

For insight into how to give constructive feedback, we can look again to management guru Marshall Goldsmith. As Goldsmith, a world-renowned author, teacher, and coach, puts it:

Providing feedback has long been considered to be an essential skill for leaders. As they strive to achieve the goals of the organization, employees need to know how they are doing. They need to know if their performance is in line with what their leaders expect. They need to learn what they have done well and what they need to change. There is a fundamental problem with all types of feedback: it focuses on the past, on what has already occurred—not on the infinite variety of opportunities that can happen in the future. As such, feedback can be limited and static, as opposed to expansive and dynamic.[2]

Goldsmith thinks that we all—as individuals or members of teams and organizations—spend far too much time dwelling on the mistakes of the past, playing Monday morning quarterback if you will, at the expense of thinking of what we could be doing better in the future. To illustrate this principle, Goldsmith in an issue of *Fast Company* retells an ancient parable about two monks strolling by a stream on their way home to the monastery. As they made their way, the monks were startled to come upon a young woman in a bridal gown, sitting by the stream and crying softly. Tears rolled down her cheeks as she gazed across the water. She needed to cross to get to her wedding, but she was fearful that she might ruin her beautiful handmade gown. In this particular sect, monks were prohibited from touching women. But one of the monks was filled with compassion for the bride. Ignoring the sanction, he hoisted the woman on his shoulders and carried her across the stream. She smiled and bowed with gratitude as he noisily splashed his way back across to rejoin his companion.

The second monk was livid. "How could you do that?" he scolded. "You know we are forbidden even to touch a woman, much less pick one up and carry her around!" The offending monk listened in silence to a stern lecture that lasted all the way back to the monastery. His mind wandered as he felt the warm sunshine and listened to the birds singing. After returning to the monastery, he fell asleep for a few hours. He was jostled and awakened in the middle of the night by his fellow monk. "How could you carry that woman?" his agitated friend cried out. "Someone else could have helped her across the stream. You were a bad monk!" "What woman?" the tired monk inquired groggily. "Don't you even remember? That woman you carried across the stream," his colleague snapped. "Oh, her," laughed the sleepy monk. "I only carried her across the stream. You carried her all the way back to the monastery." The learning point is simple: Leave it at the stream.

To help us "leave it at the stream," then, Goldsmith, along with his colleague Jon Katzenbach, has developed a process they call *feed-forward*. Rather than dwell on past events, feed-forward focuses on making suggestions for taking future action. "In practicing feed-forward, coworkers are taught to ask for suggestions for the future, listen to ideas, and just say thank you," says Goldsmith. "No one is allowed to critique suggestions or to bring up the past."[3] That means that rather than blaming or pointing the finger at past actions, feed-forward becomes a collaborative effort between individuals, teams, and organizations to focus on the most effective ways to collect credit for future successes. The result is that we begin to focus on statements such as, "Let me ask you what we can do better," rather than the same old pattern of, "Let me tell you what you did wrong." By changing the focus from accusations about the past to suggestions for the future, the intention is to reduce defensiveness and increase openness to learning and change.

TAILOR YOUR STYLE

Though it may seem burdensome, you are well advised as a manager to consider the ways in which it might be helpful to adapt your attributional and communication style to the individuals who work for you. As we have seen, different employees will inevitably have different expectations about, and reactions to, credit and blame due to family, cultural, or generational differences. Take into account how people's early life experiences, gender, and culture might make them more or less responsive to certain kinds of credit and blame. Just as with any other workplace relationship, try to take an open-minded, hypothesis-testing, and scientific approach, seeing what works for different people in different situations.

FIGHT GROUPTHINK

As a leader, it's important to keep on the lookout for groupthink in order to counteract it. There are various strategies for doing so. First of all, when presiding over a group that is going to make a decision, have the group members reach independent judgments before convening to discuss those judgments or to have them presented to you. For example, in interviewing a job candidate, make sure everyone reaches their own independent opinion before you and they get together to discuss the candidate. This will help to prevent social pressures and group tendencies from causing social "contagion" and tainting the judgment of your team. As James Surowiecki argued, citing Irving Janis, groups display more "wisdom" when people reach independent judgments than when they try to second-guess what others are going to believe or which points of view they believe others will support. In such cases, the group may drive to a metaphorical Abilene, where no one really wants to go.

Secondly, as a leader you can require the team to structure counterarguments and assign devil's advocates to make sure that the group thoroughly considers alternative explanations before assigning credit or blame. Encourage all members of the group to speak openly and candidly, sharing their true points of view without fear of being blamed by the group for speaking up. It's also helpful to create mechanisms for teams to get feedback from other teams, so that team perceptions can be benchmarked and reality-tested against others', preventing any one team from becoming too isolated or insular.

If things go wrong, discourage the group from scapegoating individual members. Instead, encourage them to reflect on systemic structural, cultural, or process issues that may have created or exacerbated problems. Reward "truth" for speaking to "power," and openly debate fundamental strategic assumptions and paradigms, no matter how much the team or organization may be committed to, or invested in, these assumptions and paradigms. Also, encourage the group to conduct "process checks" and to reflect on its own perspectives and performance, so that the group too can take an adaptive approach, and restructure and reconfigure itself as circumstances change.

FOCUS ON SYSTEMS AND SITUATIONS

In your role as an executive or manager, it's much more important and helpful to diagnose systemic weaknesses or breakdowns than to engage in witch-hunts or the proverbial "search for the guilty." Make sure organizational evaluation and appraisal systems take situations into account, and monitor the feedback that people receive from others in order to ensure that results are not overattributed to their personality or to their group membership. Establish open, candid discussions about how performance was impacted by situational factors for better or worse, and what can be done to improve results in the future. When evaluating managers and employees, make sure to balance a focus on their individual performance with a focus on their roles and the situations in which they are working. As suggested earlier, it's useful to give employees and managers the opportunity to convey their perspective on the contextual factors that either helped or hindered their performance.

If a person's performance is not up to expectations, or if challenges arise in workplace relationships, investigate whether the issue reflects larger organizational problems before concluding that it is personal or personality-based. Consider not just the interpersonal tensions between individuals but also the potential inherent tensions between the priorities of their respective roles or departments. If a group develops internal conflict, consider whether interpersonal issues are the effect, rather than the cause, of the group's difficulties. Examine whether the group has structural issues, whether roles need to be defined or redefined, or whether the group needs more or different support from you or the organization.

In addition to considering structural factors, it is also a good idea to consider incentives. Evaluate formal and informal reward systems on an ongoing basis to ensure that there is an alignment between organizational strategy and the employee behaviors that the organization credits or blames. Beware of "rewarding A while hoping for B." If you find that you are always asking for "B" and receiving "A," this may be an indication that people are actually being rewarded for doing "A," or perhaps even afraid of being blamed for doing "B." As a leader, you can open up constructive discussions about what people view as their incentives, and may be able to modify incentives to more closely align positive outcomes with desired behaviors.

If you observe "us versus them" dynamics, explore whether there are real or perceived incentives for noncooperative behavior. If there are, try to reduce them in both substantive and symbolic ways, while simultaneously providing greater incentives for individuals and groups to collaborate with one another.

GET, AND KEEP, PEOPLE WHO DON'T THROW OTHERS UNDER THE BUS

When hiring for your team or organization, pay attention to how job candidates, whether internal or external, talk about credit and blame in interviews, and when checking references ask about the candidate's credit and blame style. Candidates who take a balanced and nuanced view of credit and blame are likely to make better leaders, teammates, and subordinates. Candidates who seem biased and self-serving are likely to encounter difficulties in both leading and collaborating. Hire people who can take a self-aware, nuanced, open approach to their personal performance. Avoid candidates who evaluate themselves in a self-serving, black-and-white manner, or who have left a trail of "blameful" wreckage in their wake at past jobs.

If you manage managers, make sure you have visibility into how these managers are assigning credit or blame to the people who work for them, both formally and informally. If you learn that their staffs feel like they are not fairly credited, or feel unfairly blamed, it may be helpful to coach the manager on his or her method of conveying credit and blame. Perhaps you can add some useful perspective about how the manager is being perceived, and what he or she could potentially do to demonstrate a more open, effective credit and blame style. Even if you manage people who do not manage others, coaching them about how they are reacting can be invaluable as they learn and grow professionally. If people are not responsive about the degree and kind of feedback that they are providing to others, this may be an early indication of bigger problems down the road.

CREATE JOINT ACCOUNTABILITIES

In addition to disincentivizing competition and incentivizing collaboration, "superordinate goals" and joint accountabilities can help bring teams together and end intergroup recrimination and blame, as they did for the Eagles and the Rattlers in Sherif's Robber's Cave Experiment and for Carlos Ghosn's teams at Nissan. Giving members of different departments the opportunity to work together on cross-functional teams encourages shared responsibility and accountability for performance and results. The same approach that works with feuding teams can also work with feuding individuals. As a leader, you can create mechanisms for holding people responsible in a fair and productive way.

As I described in the case of Spritz Co., one best practice is to map out processes and create objective metrics, so that teams can be held individually and collectively accountable for performance, results, and solving problems rather than falling into the trap of mutual accusations and blame.

ESTABLISH A SAFE BUT NOT OVERLY COMFORTABLE ENVIRONMENT AND REWARD PEOPLE FOR STEPPING UP TO TAKE BLAME

I've heard Amy Edmondson talk about the helpful distinction between a "safe" environment and a "comfortable" one. In a safe environment, people will feel empowered and authorized to speak up and admit mistakes without undue fear of reprisal or punishment. However, this does not mean that the environment is so comfortable that there are no consequences to having made a mistake. Great leaders create environments that are safe enough for people to speak up, but not ones where people take a lackadaisical approach to their work. In order to create this kind of environment, as a boss you can and should reward people who assign credit and blame in an adaptive manner congruent with the organization's stated values and desired culture, especially those who take responsibility and blame when appropriate. Do not reward or promote those whose patterns of credit and blame are rigid and contrary to the organization's desired culture, especially those who do not accept responsibility for their own mistakes or oversights. Credit members of your team or staff who step forward to take blame, as Wernher von Braun did when he sent the champagne to the engineer, and discourage people from concealing mistakes or claiming too much credit.

WRITE A "USER'S MANUAL" BEFORE STARTING A NEW JOB

As we discussed in chapter 6, miscommunications between leaders or bosses and their subordinates are very common. When you start a new job, in addition to all the anxieties and stress of a career transition, you have entered a particularly tenuous time when credit and blame can either go right, or terribly wrong, setting the stage for success or derailment. Even for bosses who happen to come from the same cultural background as their new staff, there is still a high risk of cross-cultural miscommunication, even if the "culture" is not national or ethnic but simply that of the boss's last place of employment. As the new manager and his or her new team size each other up, all kinds of assumptions and biases can negatively impact the relationship, causing the kinds of *mondegreens* we saw in chapter 6. For example, if you ask a lot of questions about "how things are done around here," your staff may worry that there is skepticism or suspicion behind your questions. Based on this perception, the staff may begin to feel and act defensive, and may actually cause you to become distrustful, thereby confirming their initial negative assumptions and creating a negative spiral.

In 2003, *Wall Street Journal* career columnist Joann Lublin published an article titled "Job Candidates Get a Manual from Boss: 'How to Handle Me,'" in which she cited a concept developed by Laurence Stybel, co-founder of Stybel Peabody & Lincolnshire. In short, the idea is for the new manager to create a document, a kind of "User's Manual," to introduce themselves to their new staff. The benefit of this document is that it provides an opportunity for the new manager to accelerate the getting-to-know-you process with the new team, and to prevent mondegreens and greatly reduce the likelihood of negative, self-fulfilling relationship dynamics occurring.[4]

In the hypothetical example just mentioned, where your questions are interpreted as skeptical or suspicious, a User's Manual might have allowed you to clarify: "My style is to ask a lot of questions. I've been told in the past that these questions make me come across as critical of, or overly concerned about, the work that my staff is doing. In fact, that's not the case. I'm just curious about a lot of things and like to have a clear line of sight into the details of what you're working on." You might also provide some additional details, such as, for example, "I'm British, so I tend to be reserved. To Americans, this might make me seem aloof, when in fact I'm a very friendly, approachable person." Opening up this kind of dialogue can help prevent incorrect or unhelpful attributions by the new staff, and can obviate the potentially negative cycles of projective identification, self-fulfilling prophecies, and "set up to fail syndrome" we discussed in chapter 4.

A FINAL THOUGHT

Credit and blame present lifelong and career-long challenges for all of us. A philosopher once said: "There are two kinds of pain in life: avoidable pain and unavoidable pain. The only kind of pain that is avoidable is the pain we cause ourselves and others in unsuccessfully trying to avoid unavoidable pain." There is no question that the blame game can be painful for all of us at times, when we don't receive the credit that we deserve, or when we are unfairly blamed for things that are clearly not our fault. However, what we do in response can often become more important and problematic than the original issue. We may yield to temptation and fall back into bad habits, reacting in a quick, impulsive, and self-serving way, and make things worse, causing ourselves and others additional, avoidable pain. My goal in writing this book is for the ideas, research, and stories I've presented to help you and your organization or team avoid some of the unnecessary pain in the workplace. Ultimately, the dynamics of credit and blame will either keep us stuck in the present or the past, or they will help us to adapt and evolve, enabling us to focus on the future. The only winning move in the blame game is not to play.

I hope that in these pages you have gained new ways of thinking about how individual psychology, relationships between people, dynamics within and between teams, organizational cultures, and leadership all come together in the crucible of credit and blame. May this knowledge help you move forward in your job and your career toward a future of learning and accomplishment.

Acknowledgments

It is ironic, given the topic, that it's impossible for me to give due credit to all of the people who helped me launch my career and write this book. I wish I could fully thank each and every one of these colleagues, collaborators, family members, friends, mentors, and teachers individually, but to do so would have taken up the whole book. It's also nearly impossible to place anybody into a single one of these categories. All of the blame for errors, omissions, or any other shortcomings of this book is, of course, mine, and mine alone.

THE DATTNER CONSULTING TEAM

Julia Bindman, Charles Bush, Allison Dunn, Geraldine Grossman, Mark Horney, Hilary Pearl, and Emily Rothenberg.

MENTORS AND TEACHERS

Seymour Adler, Harold Goldstein, the late Larry Gould, Madeline Heilman, Larry Hirschhorn, Harvey Hornstein, Jim Krantz, Ellen Langer, Christopher Lehmann-Haupt, Raleigh Mayer, Brian Schwartz, Zur Shapira, Kerry Sulkowicz, Jeff Vancouver, and Howard Welsh.

ACKNOWLEDGMENTS

COLLEAGUES AND COLLABORATORS

Victoria Alzapiedi, Nancy Ancowitz, Dominick Anfuso, Mila Baker, Natalie Baumgartner, Tyler Benjamin, LeAnne Bennett, Lisa Barse Bernstein, Julie Betancur, Nikki Bethel, Kim Bors, Lee Botnick, Clif Boutelle, Maggie Bradley, George Bradt, Meg Bradt, Suzanne Brienza, Janet Brownlee, Dina Brughmans, Roger Brunswick, Michel Buffet, Lue Calandra, Joan Caruso, Ken Caruso, Bill Cassidy, Ellis Chase, Hannah Chase, Ewa Cichostepska, Karen Claro, Ross Clinchy, Barry Cohen, Ron Cohen, Michelle Conlin, Paul Connolly, Gokben Cramer, Kevin Cuthbert, Laura Daley, Lynne Davidson, Bert Davis, Daniel Debow, Ann Demarais, Tracy Dobbins, Christine Donnelly, Tracy Duberman, Denise Duca, B. Alan Echtenkamp, Scott Eggebeen, Kimberly Fey, Peter Finkelstein, Judith Finley, Tina Finnegan, Shane Fleming, Nona Footz, Amy Frankel, John Fulkerson, Anika Gakovic, Kathleen Gioffre, Judith Glaser, Robert Goldrich, Mariko Gordon, Daniel Grady, Edy Greenblatt, Jane Greenman, Adam Grossberg, Beth Gullette, Deb Hamby, Gary Hayes, Sarah Henry, Joyce Hogan, Steve Inskeep, Kristen Ireland, Mercedes Jahn, Trish Jeffers, Rob Kaiser, Miriam Katowitz, Liz Katz, Kristen Kirkland, Nick Klute, Lisa Kohn, Leon Kraig, Mary Kralj, Anat Lechner, Tien-Yi Lee, Karen Lefebrve, Erin Lehman, Danielle Leone, Robert Levine, Sara Littauer, Greg Lituchy, Henry Lodge, Marc Lowenberg, Joann Lublin, Marilyn Machlowitz, Jane Maksoud, Marc Maltz, Kevin McAliley, Scott McElhone, Annie McKee, Robyn McLeod, Art Malen, Lola Mason, Connie Miller, Lori Monson, Renee Montagne, Bill Morin, Tim Morin, Anne Moretti, Mark Nicholls, Ed Piccolino, Alexandra Pisano, Jodi Rabinowitz, Jane Rhee, Doug Riddle, Joanna Rock, Denise Roistacher, Catherine Ruvolo, Jessica Saltz, Susan Sandlund, Steve Schloss,

ACKNOWLEDGMENTS

Al Schnur, Lisa Sharaby, Christine Sheedy, Mani Shukla, Jeff Silberstein, Beth Silver, Karlin Sloan, Jessica Smith, Rich Smith, Frances Soliven, Maryanne Spatola, Connie Steensma, Mindy Stern, Bob Sutton, Anna Tavis, Ron Thomas, Oriana Tickell de Castello, Kip Trum, Lorraine Twomley, Annamarie Valerio, Vera Vitels, Michael Vom Brocke, Ruth Wageman, Vicki Walia, Rachel Wallins, Lee Wanveer, Kittie Watson, Conny Wittke, Elizabeth Wood, Simon Ziff and Kathy Zukof.

FAMILY AND FRIENDS

Yacine Ait-Sahalia, Davina Askin, Angela Attia, Uri Attia, Melissa Bachner, Upasna Bajaj, Cindy Bates, Josh Bazell, Rebecca Bazell, Julie Bitton, David Bleckner, Amanda Boren, Steve Boren, Justine Borer, Charles Both, Deborah Both, Jonathan Both, Laura Rebekah Both, Lael Brodsky, Peter Brodsky, Kate Eberle Bush, Linda Chauncey, Tom Chauncey, Anne Corbin, Alexandra Cordero, Kristina Cordero, Rebecca Crotts, Amy Davidson, Naphtali Deutsch, Seth Dinnerman, Maude DiVittis, Jewel Donohue, Judith Dunn, Mark Dunn, Marcie Elias, Felecia Wein Ettenberg, Martin Ettenberg, Dan Fisher, Geoff Fletcher, Joanna Fried, Anna Suh Garon, Ross Garon, Meg Gleason, Meredith Goldsmith, Stephanie Jo Gomez, Claudia Gonson, Jon Gould, Malya Gross, Eliot Hamlisch, Lisa Krieger Hamlisch, Matt Hoffman, Evan Houtrides, Jina Hwang, Jeff Kaufman, Jennifer Kaufman, Julian Kaufmann, Wendy Kleinman, Barry Langman, Sam Linsky, Tori Luby, Barbara Luftman, Jack Luftman, Daniel Magnus, Sophie Meunier, Jessica Meyer, Josephine P. Mogelof, Steve Murray, Orla NicDomhnaill, Elizabeth O'Neill, Lynn Oberlander, Annie Murphy Paul, Dina Pruzansky, Ripa Rashid, Joe Rhinewine, Katherine Rhinewine, Natalie Robins, Jamie Rosen, Mariana

ACKNOWLEDGMENTS

Rosen, Kevin Schlanger, Suzanne Schlanger, Julie Schonfeld, Andreas Seuffert, Erin Bertocci Seuffert, Libby Shani, Josselyn Simpson, Hollie Teslow, Gigi Toussie, Lalith Urs, Joe Vance, Solita Wakefield, Jessica Waldman, Stuart Waldman, Marcelle Walker, Brian Welle, Jason White, Leslie Wilson, Judy Wong, Tai Wong, and Jesse Zanger.

EXTRA CREDIT

My parents, for their love, as well as their constant support and encouragement.

My sister for her love and all of the lessons she has taught me about fairness.

Allison Dunn, my business partner, who came along and turned Dattner Consulting from an idea into an organization.

Amy Edmondson, who provided invaluable assistance and research for the organizational culture chapter.

Jennifer Gates, my agent at Zachary Schuster Harmsworth. Without her and Esmond Harmsworth, this book would have never been proposed, much less written. Sine Jen Non.

Richard Hackman, who introduced me to organizational psychology when I had the great fortune to take his excellent course, "The Social Psychology of Organizations" as an undergraduate twenty years ago, and who has provided much guidance and wisdom since then.

Robert Hogan, a mentor, teacher, colleague, and friend, who provided me with invaluable research, writings, theory, and insight for the personality and personality types chapter.

Emily Loose, my amazing editor at Free Press, who believed in this project from the beginning and carefully shaped this book from the raw ideas it began as into the final work product it became.

ACKNOWLEDGMENTS

And, last but by no means least, much credit to my talented co-writer, Darren Dahl, without whom this book would not exist. Over the last two years, Darren and I have worked closely together almost every day as partners in this endeavor. He never once blamed me for being vague, changing things around, or asking him to do more research and writing than was reasonable.

Notes

INTRODUCTION

1. The account of U.S. Air Flight 1549 is taken from Chesley Sullenberger and Jeffrey Zaslow, *Highest Duty* (New York: William Morrow, 2009), and William Langewiesche, *Fly by Wire* (New York: Farrar, Straus & Giroux, 2009).
2. Joyce Hogan, Robert Hogan, and Robert Kaiser, *Management Derailment*, in Sheldon Zedeck, ed., *APA Handbook of Industrial and Organizational Psychology*, vol. 3 (Washington, DC: *American Psychological Association*, 2010), pp. 555–76.
3. Jean Brittain Leslie and Ellen Van Velsor, *A Look at Derailment Today: North America and Europe* (Greensboro, NC: CCL Press, 1996).
4. Howard Tennen and Glenn Affleck, "Blaming others for threatening events," *Psychological Bulletin* (1990), pp. 209–32.
5. George Vaillant, *Adaptation to Life* (Boston: Little, Brown, 1977), p. 162.
6. Leslie Phillips, *Human Adaptation and Its Failures* (New York: Academic Press, 1968).
7. John Seabrook, "The Flash of Genius," *The New Yorker*, January 11, 1993.
8. Steven Pinker, *How the Mind Works* (New York: W. W. Norton & Co., 1999).
9. Matt Ridley, *The Origins of Virtue: Human Instincts and the Evolution of Cooperation* (New York: Viking, 2007), p. 62.

CHAPTER 1: The Nature of Credit and Blame

1. Jon Gould, *Can't Buy Me Love: The Beatles, Britain and America* (New York: Three Rivers Press, 2007).
2. "Records: Mix-Master to the Beatles," *Time*, June 16, 1967.
3. Sarah Brosnan and Frans de Waal, "Monkeys reject unequal pay," *Nature*, 425, September 18, 2003.
4. Ridley, *The Origins of Virtue: Human Instincts and the Evolution of Cooperation*, p. 62.
5. John Stacey Adams, "Inequity in social exchange," *Advances in Experimental Social Psychology* (1965), pp. 335–43.
6. Daniel Gilbert, *Stumbling on Happiness* (New York: Knopf, 2006), p. 98.
7. Chun Siong Soon, et al., "Unconscious determinants of free decisions in the human brain," *Nature Neuroscience*, April 13, 2008.
8. Werner Güth, Rolf Schmittberger, and Bernd Schwarze, "An experimental analysis of ultimatum bargaining," *Journal of Economic Behavior and Organization*, vol. 3, no. 4 (December 1982), pp. 367–88.
9. Anthony Greenwald, "The totalitarian ego," *American Psychologist* (July 1980), p. 605.
10. Steven Pinker, *The Blank Slate* (New York: Penguin, 2002), p. 265.
11. Bertrand Russell, *Sceptical Essays* (London: Routledge, 2004), p. 16.
12. Justin Kruger and David Dunning, "Unskilled and unaware of it: How difficulties in recognizing one's own incompetence lead to inflated self-assessments," *Journal of Personality and Social Psychology* (December 1999), pp. 1121–34.
13. Gerald R. Salancik and James R. Meindl, "Corporate attributions as strategic illusions of management control," *Administrative Science Quarterly* (1984), pp. 238–54.
14. Edward G. Rogoff, Myung-Soo Lee, and Dong-Churl Suh, "Who done it? Attributions by entrepreneurs and experts of the factors that cause and impede small business success," *Journal of Small Business Management* (2004), pp. 364–76.
15. Kathryn Saulnier and Daniel Perlman, "The actor-observer bias is alive and well in prison: A sequel to Wells," *Personality and Social Psychology Bulletin*, vol. 7, no. 4 (December 1981), pp. 559–64.
16. See wsj.com/article/NA_WSJ_PUB:SB122178211966454607.html, accessed August 31, 2010.

17. Francine Patterson and Eugene Linden, *The Education of Koko* (New York: Holt, Rinehart & Winston, 1981).

18. See websters-online-dictionary.org/definitions/SCAPEGOAT?cx=partner -pub-0939450753529744%3Av0qd01-tdlq&cof=FORID%3A9&ie= UTF-8&q=SCAPEGOAT.

19. James George Frazer, *The Golden Bough: A Study in Magic and Religion* (1890; New York: The Macmillan Co., 1922), p. 22.

20. Julian Barnes, *Nothing to Be Frightened Of* (New York: Alfred A. Knopf, 2008), p. 58.

21. See Mary Beth Norton, *In the Devil's Snare* (New York: Alfred A. Knopf, 2002); Robert Rapley, *Witch Hunts* (Montreal: McGill-Queen's University Press, 2007); and Frances Hill, *The Salem Witch Trials Reader* (New York: Da Capo Press, 2000), p. xvii.

22. Edmund Andrews and Peter Baker, "A.I.G. Planning Huge Bonuses After $170 Billion Bailout," *New York Times*, March 14, 2009.

23. Sheryl Gay Stolberg, "The Art of Political Distraction," *New York Times*, March 21, 2009.

24. Elizabeth Rauber, "Cal Study: Human Social Behavior Influences Corporate Witch Hunts," *San Francisco Business Times*, July 17, 2008.

25. Cari Tuna, "Some Firms Cut Costs Without Resorting to Layoffs," *Wall Street Journal*, December 15, 2008.

26. Anthony G. Greenwald, Debbie E. McGhee, and Jordan L. K. Schwartz, "Measuring individual differences in implicit cognition: The Implicit Association Test," *Journal of Personality and Social Psychology*, vol. 74, no. 6 (June 1998), pp. 1464–80.

27. "'As the World Turns' Villainess Will Miss Fans, Family," National Public Radio, *Morning Edition*, December 14, 2009.

28. Official Jeopardy Page: www.jeopardy.com/showguide/bios/alextrebek/.

29. Campbell Robertson, "Steven Dorfman, 48, Quirky Writer for 'Jeopardy!'" *New York Times*, January 9, 2004.

30. Lee D. Ross, Teresa M. Amabile, and Julia L. Steinmetz, "Social roles, social control, and biases in social-perception processes," *Journal of Personality and Social Psychology*, vol. 35, no. 7 July (1977), pp. 485–94.

31. Joseph Campbell, *The Hero with a Thousand Faces* (New York: Pantheon, 1949).

NOTES

CHAPTER 2: The Nurture of Credit and Blame

1. Charles Tilly, "Memorials to credit and blame," *The American Interest*, vol. 3, no. 5 (May–June 2008).
2. Adam Gostick and Chester Elton, *The Carrot Principle: How Great Managers Use Employee Recognition* (New York: Free Press, 2009).
3. Marilyn Lopes, "Can You Praise Children Too Much?" *CareGiver News* (August 1993) p. 1 (Amherst, MA: University of Massachusetts Cooperative Extension).
4. Jeffrey Zaslow, "The Most-Praised Generation Goes to Work," *Wall Street Journal*, May 18, 2007.
5. Melissa L. Kamins, and Carol S. Dweck, "Person versus process praise and criticism: Implications for contingent self-worth and coping," *Developmental Psychology*, vol. 35, no. 3 (1999), pp. 835–47.
6. Michelle Conlin, "I'm a Bad Boss? Blame My Dad," *BusinessWeek*, May 10, 2004.
7. Sarah Kershaw, "Family and Office Roles Mix," *New York Times*, December 3, 2008.
8. Martin Seligman, Lyn Abramson, and Amy Semmel, "Depressive attributional style," *Journal of Abnormal Psychology*, vol. 88, no. 3 (1979), pp. 242–47.
9. Bernard Weiner, *An Attributional Theory of Motivation and Emotion* (New York: Springer-Verlag, 1986).
10. Jennifer Lau, Frühling Rijsdijk, and Thalia C. Eley, "I think, therefore I am: A twin study of attributional style in adolescents," *Journal of Child Psychology and Psychiatry* (August 2005), pp. 696–703.
11. Jill Hooley, "How Depression Lingers," *Harvard Magazine* (July–August 2009).
12. Ibid.
13. Christopher Peterson, Steven Maier, and Martin Seligman, *Learned Helplessness: A Theory for the Age of Personal Control* (New York: Oxford University Press, 1995).
14. Daniel Goleman, "Women's Depression Rate Is Higher," *New York Times*, December 6, 1990.
15. Stephanie Pappas, "Women Intensely Dissatisfied with Pay Gap," *BusinessNewsDaily*, July 26, 2010.
16. Peggy Klaus, *Brag!* (New York: Warner Business Books, 2003), p. 17.
17. Scott N. Taylor, "It may not be what you think: Gender differences in

predicting emotional and social competence," *Presentation at National Academy of Management Conference*, Chicago, cited in www.aomonline .org/aom.asp?ID=251&page_ID=224&pr_id=417.

18. Geert Hofstede, *Culture's Consequences: Comparing values, behaviors, institutions, and organizations across nations*, 2d ed. (Thousand Oaks, CA: Sage Publications, 2001).

19. Malcolm Gladwell, *Outliers* (New York: Little, Brown, 2008).

20. Constantine Sedikides, Lowell Gaertner, and Yoshiyasu Toguchi, "Pan-cultural self-enhancement," *Journal of Personality and Social Psychology* (January 2003), pp. 60–79.

21. Tanya Menon, et al., "Culture and the construal of agency: Attribution to individual versus group dispositions," *Journal of Personality and Social Psychology* (January 1999), pp. 701–17.

22. Jesse McKinley, "FYI: Big Whale, Strong Java," *New York Times*, July 14, 1996.

23. John Rawls, *A Theory of Justice* (Cambridge, MA: Harvard University Press, 1971).

CHAPTER 3: Typecasting Blame

1. Annie Murphy Paul, *The Cult of Personality: How Personality Tests Are Leading Us to Miseducate Our Children, Mismanage Our Companies, and Misunderstand Ourselves* (New York: Free Press, 2005).

2. Dan McAdams, "A psychology of the stranger," *Psychological Inquiry* (1994), pp. 145–48.

3. Daniel Goleman, *Working with Emotional Intelligence* (New York: Bantam Books, 1998).

4. Gregor Domes, et al., "Oxytocin improves 'mind-reading' in humans," *Biological Psychiatry*, vol. 61, no. 6 (March 2007), pp. 731–33.

5. John Tierney, "Hallucinogens Have Doctors Tuning In Again," *New York Times*, April 11, 2010.

6. See www.mdma.net/alexander-shulgin/mdma.html.

7. Paul Costa, Jr., and Robert McCrae, *Revised NEO Personality Inventory (NEO-PI-R) and NEO Five-Factor Inventory (NEO-FFI) Manual* (Odessa, FL: Psychological Assessment Resources, 1992). IPIP online test result output.

8. Nancy Ancowitz, *Self-Promotion for Introverts* (New York: McGraw-Hill, 2010), p. 3.

9. For a free, online self-assessment of your personality as measured by the Big Five and its subfactors, go to www.personal.psu.edu/j5j/IPIP/ ipipneo120.htm. There are 120 questions on this assessment, and for each one the participant fills out a five-point scale of how accurate an item is in describing him or her, ranging from "very inaccurate" to "very accurate"—for example: "Am afraid to draw attention to myself," "Get irritated easily," or "Boast about my virtues." See also www.psychometric -success.com/personality-tests/personality-tests-big-5-aspects.htm.

10. *Hogan Development Survey Manual*, Hogan Assessment Systems, 1997.

11. Personal e-mail communication from Robert Hogan, July 6, 2009. Robert Hogan was enormously generous and helpful in assisting with the development of the personality types based on his extensive research and experience as the leading test developer in the country. Note that the classification of types into categories, for example, "reserved" under "impunitive" rather than "extrapunitive," have not been fully empirically or statistically established. Robert Hogan suggested "reserved" might actually fit under "extrapunitive" from a statistical point of view, although he agreed that conceptually it may arguably be closer to "impunitive."

The three categories into which the eleven dysfunctional personality types can be placed are derived from the "Rosenzweig Picture-Frustration Study," developed by psychologist Saul Rosenzweig in the 1940s. Although called a study, it is actually a projective test that was designed to assess aggression. It consists of twenty-four cards which feature two people in different, "frustrating" situations, one as the "antagonist" and the other the "protagonist," each with their own "speech balloon." The antagonist's speech bubble is filled in; the protagonist's is not. The subject is asked to imagine himself as the protagonist, and to fill in the protagonist's speech balloon in the way he would react in that scenario. Depending on the subject's response, the assessor makes a number of classifications, including whether the subject denies blame, blames the other person, or blames himself. Although there has long been debate about the validity of projective tests, and it is debatable which of the eleven types fits best into them, the three conceptual categories are still useful in thinking about the dynamics of blame.

12. An excellent source for further information about dysfunctional personalities used for background on the dysfunctional types is Theodore Millon, et al., *Personality Disorders in Modern Life*, 2nd ed. (New York: John Wiley & Sons, 2004).

13. Jim Collins, *Good to Great* (New York: HarperBusiness, 2001).

CHAPTER 4: Situational Awareness

1. William Poundstone, *Prisoner's Dilemma* (New York: Doubleday, 1992).

2. Robert Axelrod, *The Evolution of Cooperation*, rev. ed. (New York: Basic Books, 2006).

3. William Safire, "On Language: Groupthink," *New York Times*, August 8, 2004: nytimes.com/2004/08/08/magazine/the-way-we-live-now-8-8-04-on-language-groupthink.html.

4. James Surowiecki, *The Wisdom of Crowds* (New York: Anchor Books, 2005), p. 36.

5. Solomon Asch "Opinions and Social Pressure," *Scientific American*, 193 (1955), pp. 31–35.

6. Jerry Harvey, *The Abilene Paradox and Other Meditations on Management* (San Francisco: Jossey-Bass, 1988).

7. Carlos Ghosn, "Saving the Business Without Losing the Company," *Harvard Business Review* (January 2002), 80(1), pp. 3–11.

8. Thomas Pettigrew, "The ultimate attribution error: Extending Allport's cognitive analysis of prejudice personality," *Social Psychology Bulletin*, vol. 5, no. 4 (October 1979), pp. 461–76.

9. John Tierney, "Deep Down, We Can't Fool Even Ourselves," *New York Times*, July 1, 2008.

10. Albert Hastorf and Hadley Cantril, "They saw a game: A case study," *Journal of Abnormal and Social Psychology*, (January 1954), 49(1) pp. 129–34.

11. Muzafer Sherif, et al., *Intergroup Conflict and Cooperation: The Robber's Cave Experiment* (Norman, OK: University of Oklahoma Book Exchange, 1961).

12. Tim Arrango, "How the AOL–Time Warner Merger Went So Wrong," *New York Times*, January 10, 2010.

13. Patricia Sellars, "Ted Turner is a worried man," *Fortune*, May 26, 2003: http://money.cnn.com/magazines/fortune/fortune_archive/2003/05/26/343113/index.htm, accessed on October 4, 2010.

14. Ibid.

15. Robert Rosenthal and Lenore Jacobson, *Pygmalion in the Classroom* (New York: Irvington Publishers, 1992).

16. Saul Kassin, Steven Fein, and Hazel Rose Markus, *Social Psychology*, 7th ed. (New York: Houghton Mifflin, 2008), pp. 122–24.

17. Jean-François Manzoni and Jean-Louis Barsoux, *The Set-Up-to-Fail Syn-*

drome: How Good Managers Cause Great People to Fail (Cambridge, MA: HBS Press, 2002), p. 6.

18. See Otto Kernberg, "Projection and projective identification: Developmental and clinical aspects," *Journal of the American Psychoanalytic Association*, vol. 35, no. 4 (1987), pp. 795–819.

19. For a detailed explanation of projective identification, see Leonard Horwitz, "Projective identification in dyads and groups," *International Journal of Group Psychotherapy*, vol. 33, no. 3 (1983), pp. 259–75.

20. *This Emotional Life, Part I*, PBS, January 4, 2010; www.thisemotionallife .com.

CHAPTER 5: Cultures of Blame

1. *Saturday Night Live*, October 24, 1992; snltranscripts.jt.org/92/92djiffy .phtml.

2. Daniel Kahnemann and Amos Tversky, "On the psychology of prediction," *Psychological Review* (1973), pp. 237–51.

3. *National Commission on Terrorist Attacks, The 9/11 Commission Report: Final Report of the National Commission on Terrorist Attacks Upon the United States* (New York: W. W. Norton & Co., 2004), p. xv.

4. Ibid, p. 362.

5. Richard A. Posner, "The 9/11 Report: A Dissent," *New York Times*, August 29, 2004.

6. Ibid.

7. www.nasa.gov/offices/oce/appel/ask-academy/issues/ask-oce/AO_1 -6_F_mistakes.html.

8. David Koenig, "Southwest Airlines Posts 4Q, Full-Year Profit," *Associated Press*, January 21, 2010; abcnews.go.com/Business/wireStory?id=9621566.

9. Jody Hoffer Gittell, *The Southwest Airlines Way: Using the Power of Relationships to Achieve High Performance* (New York: McGraw-Hill, 2005), p. 28.

10. Ibid.

11. Jena McGregor, "How Failure Breeds Success," *BusinessWeek*, July 10, 2006.

12. Mark D. Cannon and Amy C. Edmondson, "Failing to Learn and Learning to Fail (Intelligently): How Great Organizations Put Failure to Work to Improve and Innovate," *Long Range Planning*, volume 38, issue 3, June 2005, pp. 299–319.

13. Thom Shanker, "Iran Encounter Grimly Echoes '02 War Game," *New York Times*, January 12, 2008; nytimes.com/2008/01/12/washington/12navy.html.

14. Ibid.

15. Diane Coutu, "Edgar Schein: The Anxiety of Learning—The Darker Side of Organizational Learning," *Harvard Business School Working Knowledge*, April 15, 2002.

16. Peter F. Drucker, *Innovation and Entrepreneurship: Practice and Principles* (New York: Harper & Row, 1985).

17. Cannon and Edmondson, "Failing to Learn and Learning to Fail (Intelligently)."

18. Steven Kerr, "On the Folly of Rewarding A, While Hoping for B," *Academy of Management Executive* (1995), pp. 7–14.

19. Ronald Heifetz and Marty Linsky, *Leadership on the Line* (Cambridge, MA: Harvard Business School Press, 2002).

20. Fiona Lee and Christopher Peterson, "Mea culpa: Predicting stock prices from organizational attributions," *Personality and Social Psychology Bulletin* (2004), p. 1945.

21. Ibid., p. 1647.

22. Kevin Sack, "Doctors Say 'I'm Sorry' Before 'See You in Court,'" *New York Times*, May 18, 2008.

23. Amy Edmondson, "Learning from mistakes is easier said than done: Group and organization influences on the detection and correction of human error," *Journal of Applied Behavioral Science* (1996), pp. 5–28.

24. Amy Edmondson, Michael Roberto, and Anita Tucker, "Children's Hospital and Clinics," *Harvard Business School Case Study*, November 15, 2001, pp. 6–7.

25. Ibid.

26. Ibid., p. 8.

27. Ibid., p. 9.

28. Sarah Jane Gilbert, "Do I Dare Say Something? Q & A with Amy Edmondson," *HBS Working Knowledge*, March 20, 2006.

29. Amy C. Edmondson, Corey Hajim, "Safe to Say at Prudential Financial," *Harvard Business School Publishing*, March 20, 2007.

30. Ibid., p. 8.

31. Michael Tushman and Charles A. O'Reilly III, *Winning Through Innovation* (Cambridge, MA: Harvard Business School Press, 2002), pp. 4–10.

NOTES

CHAPTER 6: Leaders Reframe Blame

1. Stephen Ambrose, *D-Day: June 6, 1944: The Climactic Battle of World War II* (New York: Simon & Schuster, 1995), p. 190.
2. David McCullough, *Truman* (New York: Simon & Schuster, 1993), p. 464.
3. Alan Axelrod, *When the Buck Stops with You* (New York: Portfolio, 2004); www.trumanlibrary.org/buckstop.htm; http://www.whitehousemuseum .org/west-wing/resolute-desk.htm.
4. See old.nationalreview.com/comment/wallison200406051905.asp; Peter Wallison, "A Man Apart: Reagan had the right principles—and he stuck to them," *National Review Online*, June 5, 2004.
5. See Andrew S. Grove, *Only the Paranoid Survive* (New York: Doubleday, 1999).
6. John Markoff, "In About-Face, Intel Will Swap Its Flawed Chip," *New York Times*, December 21, 1994; David Fritzsche, *Business Ethics: A Global and Managerial Perspective* (New York: McGraw-Hill/Irwin, 2004), p. 31; and Jim DeTar, "Intel Initiates Pentium Replacements," *Electronic News*, January 2, 1995.
7. Grove, *Only the Paranoid Survive*, p. 22.
8. Diane L. Coutu, "Edgar Schein: The Anxiety of Learning—The darker side of organizational learning," *Harvard Business Review*, April 15, 2002.
9. Collins, *Good to Great*, p. 28.
10. Ibid.
11. Amy Barrett, "Pfizer's Funk," *BusinessWeek*, February 28, 2005.
12. Edward E. Lawler III and Chris Worley, *Built to Change: How to Achieve Sustained Organizational Effectiveness* (San Francisco: Jossey-Bass, 2006), p. 129.
13. Ibid.
14. Marshall Goldsmith, "To Help Others Develop, Start with Yourself," *Fast Company*, March 1, 2004.
15. Adam Bryant, "He's Not Bill Gates, or Fred Astaire," *New York Times*, February 13, 2010.
16. Theodor W. Adorno, et al., *The Authoritarian Personality* (New York: Harper and Row, 1950).
17. Sylvia Wright, *Get Away from Me with Those Christmas Gifts* (New York: McGraw-Hill, 1957).

18. Marilyn Berger, "Isaiah Berlin, Philosopher and Pluralist, Is Dead at 88," *New York Times*, November 7, 1997.

19. Christopher Lydon, "J. Edgar Hoover Made the F.B.I. Formidable with Politics, Publicity and Results," *New York Times*, May 3, 1972.

20. Paul B. Carroll and Chunka Mui, *Billion-Dollar Lessons: What you can learn from the most inexcusable business failures of the last 25 years* (New York: Portfolio, 2008), p. 1.

21. David Freedman, "Entrepreneur of the Year," *Inc.*, January 1, 2005.

22. "Wisconsin Police Chief Tickets Himself $235," *Associated Press*, February 3, 2007.

23. Goldsmith, "To Help Others Develop, Start with Yourself."

24. Adam Bryant, "Xerox's New Chief Tries to Redefine Its Culture," *New York Times*, February 20, 2010.

25. Ibid.

26. James Chiles, *Inviting Disaster* (New York: HarperCollins, 2002), p. 278.

CHAPTER 7: Practical Approaches

1. David Rock, *Your Brain at Work* (New York: HarperBusiness, 2009).

2. www.marshallgoldsmithlibrary.com/docs/articles/Feedforward.doc.

3. Marshall Goldsmith, "Leave It at the Stream," *Fast Company*, May 1, 2004.

4. Joann Lublin, "Job Candidates Get a Manual from Boss: 'How to Handle Me,'" *Wall Street Journal*, January 7, 2003.

Index

INDEX

INDEX

INDEX

About the Authors

Ben Dattner is the founder of Dattner Consulting, LLC, an organizational development and executive coaching firm that helps corporate and nonprofit organizations sort through their credit and blame issues in order to enhance individual, team, and organizational learning and performance. His clients include companies ranging from small start-ups to global corporations, nonprofit and educational institutions, and government agencies. Dattner is also an adjunct professor at New York University, where he teaches Organizational Development in the Industrial and Organizational Psychology MA Program in the Graduate School of Arts and Sciences. He has also taught Strategic Career Management in the Executive MBA Program at NYU Stern Business School. He received a BA in psychology from Harvard College, and an MA and PhD in Industrial and Organizational Psychology from New York University. He lives in New York City and his website is www.dattnerconsulting.com.

Darren Dahl has worked as a collaborative writer and editor with several high-profile authors, including Keith McFarland on *The Breakthrough Company* (a *New York Times*, *Wall Street Journal*, and *USA Today* bestseller), and the intellectual property experts Mark Blaxill and Ralph Eckardt on their book, *The Invisible Edge* (named best strategy book of the year in 2009 by Strategy+Business). Dahl is a contributing editor at *Inc.* magazine, which he has written for since 2004. He has also written for the *New York Times* and AOL *Small Business*. He lives in Asheville, NC.